CONCORDIA
SCHOLARSHIP
Today

D1590815

GOD'S SONG
IN A NEW LAND

Lutheran Hymnals in America

Carl F. Schalk

CPH™
SAINT LOUIS

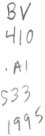

Copyright © 1995 Concordia Publishing House
3558 S. Jefferson Avenue, St. Louis, MO 63118-3968
Manufactured in the United States of America

Library of Congress Cataloging-in-Publication Data

Schalk, Carl, 1929–
    God's song in a new land: Lutheran hymnals in America / Carl F.
Schalk.
        p.   cm.   (Concordia scholarship today)
    Includes bibliographical references and index.
    ISBN 0-570-04830-3
    1. Lutheran Church—United States—Hymns—History and criticism.
    2. Hymns, English—United States—History and criticism. 3. Hymns,
German—United States—History and criticism. 4. Hymns, Scandinavian—
United States—History and criticism. I. Title. II. Series.
BV410.A1S33   1995
264' . 0417302—dc20   95-18533

1 2 3 4 5 6 7 8 9 10   04 03 02 01 00 99 98 97 96 95

GOD'S SONG
IN A NEW LAND

For Noel

Cherished spouse, partner, and fellow–singer of
God's song

Contents

CONTENTS

Foreword

God's Song in a New Land, like all volumes in the Concordia Scholarship Today series, offers useful insights as it explores, clarifies, and interprets current issues. The CST series is based on the assumption that nothing can be fully understood apart from the most momentous event of all times, the redeeming sacrifice of Jesus Christ. In response, the Christian strives and strains to express this sublime yet ineffable mystery in every available style and form.

Throughout history music has provided a supportive background for the mighty acts of God, beginning already when "the morning stars sang together and all the sons of God shouted for joy" at the creation (Job 38:7). Almost always, as we follow God through history, the sounds and songs of music are near, reinforcing and sustaining the message.

The Christian song is not always a joyful shout, sometimes even dipping down into the darkness of sorrow, realistically reflecting the essential motifs of sin and grace that accompany us throughout life. As the momentary darkness of fear and sorrow—the sorrow of sin and the separation from God—is dispelled by the Gospel, the hallelujahs and doxologies again burst forth brightly and more intensely by comparison.

For God's people the message is basic and determines the music. Historically, when the church emphasized art for art's sake, the message was diluted. At other times the message became dull and wooden as music was reduced or virtually removed from the worship service. Luther himself and his heirs have tried to strike an artistic/utilitarian balance, letting the biblical message of sin and grace be the control factor.

God's Song in a New Land sketches the degree to which

Lutherans in America have been successful in pursuing that ideal, and Carl Schalk is highly qualified to trace that history. His choral and instrumental compositions speak in the modern idiom without the harshness of less-seasoned artists, always emerging with a clear statement of the central Christian message. His music and writing reflect decades of research into the history of the church and its expressions and confessions of the day. His fresh and insightful writing and editing always display an appreciation and reverence for the text that is essential for valid interpretation. That is important for the church, which now stands in need of a recovery of the essence of worship, the mystery of the transcendental, and the sense of wonder that accompanies the contemplation of the love of God in Jesus Christ.

To meet the needs of the church, especially of the coming generation, the hymns and liturgy of the church must be of a nature that they can be assimilated over time. That can take place only if worshipers are offered appropriate hymns and liturgy. The debate as to what constitutes suitable music will never be resolved. But it also is beyond question that the rich heritage of the church will be lost unless we understand our roots and provide opportunities for exposure to what has stood the test of time.

In tracing and interpreting the history of hymnody in America, Carl Schalk has supplied background much needed for our day when a variety of incursions seem poised to distort the fundamental song of the church, the message of our salvation in Jesus Christ. Ugliness, emptiness, and absurdity have nearly become an obsession in all of the contemporary arts. The corrective can be found in contemplation and application of the record of God, the perfect creator, artist, and hymnist—in the many biblical accounts which show that God consistently encourages aesthetic expression and appreciation of his creating, redeeming, and sanctifying work among us.

The Publisher

Preface

Wherever and whenever God's people have gathered to hear his Word and celebrate the sacraments they have sung songs, songs of death and rebirth, songs of sin and salvation, songs of repentance, renewal, and new life. In Christian song words and music join together to rehearse the story of God's deliverance and to proclaim his Word to all the world.

The joining of music with Christian worship was hardly the result of historical or cultural accident. It was rather the deliberate result of the church's concern for the faith joined together with an understanding of the power of music to move our minds and hearts. In theory the wedding of music and words may appear to be a wedding of convenience; in practice it is the unavoidable result of the new life in Christ. In theory it may be possible to imagine Christian worship devoid of song; in practice the Christian community fills its gatherings with psalms, hymns, and spiritual songs. The history of the Christian worshiping community is the history of a singing and music-making community. We cannot imagine it otherwise.

From earliest times Christians gathered together their songs in collections. Some were simple, practical collections;

others were elaborate, the result of the work of skilled artisans. While collections of Christian song through the Middle Ages were ordinarily intended only for the choir, with the Lutheran Reformation of the 16th century there began the publication of a long line of collections of songs for worship for use by the people. These collections served not only the needs of corporate worship, but the devotional needs of the home and family as well.

Since the time of the Reformation, three books, it has been said, have been the principal shapers of Lutheran piety. Of these three books—the Bible, the catechism, and the hymnbook—one might reasonably argue that it is the hymnbook, certainly the most regularly and frequently encountered, that has had the most enduring and lasting influence. It is unquestionably the regular and recurrent use of hymns in worship that has shaped so much of our basic vocabulary of words, phrases, and images that have become part of both our individual and collective memory as church. Hymns implanted deep in our memory and recalled to mind in the varied situations of the Christian life, are more powerful and influential in our spiritual nurture than we might imagine. Nor was singing in Lutheran piety relegated to the Sunday gathering of the faithful. It was equally a part of Lutheran piety in the home in family and personal devotions, and hymns—at various times in Lutheran history—could be heard at work, in the fields, wherever Christians might gather. Singing hymns was an activity that permeated the Christian life day in and day out.

It was such a piety, one that treasured and nurtured Christian song, that led the early Lutheran settlers who came to North America from the various countries of the European continent to include their hymnals among the few precious possessions which they brought with them from their homeland and which they took care to pass on to those who survived them. Henry Melchior Muhlenberg, the "patriarch of American Lutheranism," was typical. Seven years after his arrival in America in 1742, he spoke about the "small chest of Bibles and hymn books which I had brought with me into this country."[1] A half-century later, in a will dated May 21, 1792, Peter Troutman Sr., a Lutheran settler in North Carolina, bequeathed to his wife, Ann Elisabeth

> her bed and furniture, one sorrel horse, one cow, her spinning wheel, one large iron pot, and one small ditto, one frying pan, one pewter dish, two plates, two spoons, one ink tray, *one psalm book*, one smoothing iron, five sheep, and one swarm of bees. . .[Emphasis added].[2]

For many early settlers the hymnal was a prized possession.

But with Lutheran immigrants coming to America from so many diverse places on the European continent, each group with its own hymn or psalm book, the confusion that followed from any attempt to use these different hymnbooks simultaneously in any particular gathering was soon evident. The desire—to be raised in turn by each successive immigrant group which came to America—was soon expressed for a single hymnbook that could be used by all Lutheran congregations. First voiced by Muhlenberg in the latter half of the 18th century, it was most clearly expressed in the Preface to the first Lutheran hymnbook fashioned in America.

> It should be noted what until now has hindered a complete unity in connection with singing in our public worship, namely the many kinds of hymnbooks, since in almost every one various little alterations have been made, and in some of which there are few hymns, in others many. *If only there were one hymnbook for all the American* [Lutheran] *congregations which would contain the best of the old and new spiritual songs, how much more convenient it would be.* [Emphasis mine][3]

It is possible to view the story of Lutheran hymnals in America through the prism of that vision of a "common hymnbook" which could be shared by all Lutherans in the New World. In a variety of ways that vision—often unawares—has for over two centuries shaped the story of Lutheran hymnals in America. The attempt to achieve that

15

vision, however, was not without its difficulties. As large numbers of immigrants began streaming to America in the 18th and 19th centuries, three rather immediate problems faced those who attempted to pursue that vision.

The first problem was that of language, a problem that resulted in the development of separate, yet related, bodies of hymnody: one for those groups that chose to remain largely German, Swedish, Norwegian, Finnish, or Danish in language and culture, the other for those who turned rather immediately to the English language. The conflict was between those who "on the one hand, would boldly adopt English in order to win America, and those who, on the other hand, feared to embrace English lest they be lost in America."[4]

The second problem was the rapid dispersement of Lutherans throughout the nation as they moved westward along the expanding frontier. This geographic expansion of Lutheranism resulted in, among other things, a proliferation of Lutheran synods, many of which felt the necessity of producing their own hymnals reflecting their particular needs, concerns, and heritage.

The third problem was the overlapping influences of Pietism, rationalism, and an amiable ecumenism. Each of these movements presented its own particular challenge. Pietism, while retaining a link with historic Lutheran hymnody, tended to emphasize the subjective character of human experience in contrast to the orthodox confessionalism of the 16th century. Rationalism frequently worked to change the content of hymnody in order to bring it into agreement with human reason. An amiable ecumenism provided an environment in which historic Lutheran hymnody often yielded to the hymnody of the surrounding denominations in America, a hymnody often characterized by a theology foreign to or at variance with understandings rooted in the Lutheran Reformation. These theological currents of the late 18th and early 19th centuries—Pietism, rationalism, and an easy-going ecumenism—tended to alter the character of Lutheran hymnody as well as the contents of its hymnals, turning the historic heritage of Lutheran hymnody into uncharted and frequently dangerous theological waters.

The influx of large numbers of German Lutheran immigrants to America beginning in the mid-19th century brought a new dimension to American Lutheran hymnody. These Lutherans—principally the Prussians under J. A. A. Grabau, the Saxons under C. F. W. Walther, and the Bavarians under the guidance of Wilhelm Loehe—came to America committed to a strict Lutheran confessionalism that was only beginning to take shape among the Lutherans who had come to America in the preceding centuries. Their confessional concern manifested itself in a variety of ways, among them the aggressive promotion of Reformation hymnody in its original texts and original melodic forms, texts and melodies that had largely been lost or radically altered in the years since the Reformation. The efforts of these groups exerted a significant influence on the subsequent history of Lutheran hymnals in America. Immigrants coming from a variety of Scandinavian countries during the 19th century brought with them their unique hymnic heritages as well.

This book is an introduction to the history of that succession of hymnals which have helped shape the piety of Lutherans in North America from 1786 until the present. These hymnbooks reflect important aspects of the story of Lutherans in America from the first "made in America" Lutheran hymnal to the most recent. This book deals, for the most part, with the *official* hymnals of the various groups that make up the history of Lutheranism in America. The story of these hymnbooks encompasses the transplanting of the hymnic heritage of the emigrants' homelands to America, the problems presented by the temptation to accommodate—or the refusal to accommodate—to the American situation, the gradual proliferation of hymnals as the Lutheran church spread throughout the expanding nation, and—in the latter 19th and 20th centuries—the movement toward consensus and consolidation, a consensus and consolidation in part given impetus to and invited by common hymnic activities among the various Lutheran bodies, and in part the result of those common activities.

There is, of course, a host of unofficial hymnals that have served Lutherans and that are an important part of the larger story: Sunday School hymnals, hymnals for youth, hymnals for schools, and other collections that attempt to fill a need presumably not met in "official" books. Such collections have often served as repositories for material not included in the official books, or—in more recent times—as experimental collections for more transient uses. The purpose of this book is to describe and evaluate the development of the official Lutheran hymnals of the various ministeriums, synods, and other official Lutheran groups in the light of the various factors that affected their development and brought them into being.

What follows here is an introduction to the succession of hymnbooks that played the major part in the development of American Lutheran hymnody from Muhlenberg's *Erbauliche Liedersammlung* (1786) to those most recently published in the latter part of the 20th century. However, to regard the succession of those Lutheran hymnbooks from Muhlenberg's time to our own as the arbitrary or capricious work of restless men and women, motivated chiefly by a spirit of aimless innovation is, I believe, a mistake. The changing shape of Lutheran hymnody in America has been rather the result of the intellectual and religious ferment of each particular age which gave it birth, and it was accepted precisely because it was in harmony with its time.

By the middle of the 20th century American Lutheranism was coming close to realizing Muhlenberg's dream as the great majority of Lutherans worked together on one hymnal that could be used by all Lutherans in America. By the end of the century, however, the achievement of that vision seemed to elude them. Muhlenberg's vision, however, is alive and well, although the particular shape it may take in the years ahead is no longer quite as clear as it was once thought to be. As America's Lutherans looks to the future of their congregational song, it is important that they look to the beginnings of their hymnody in America, but also that they look beyond to the beginnings of Lutheran hymnody in the age of the Reformation. There is much that we can learn from knowing our own story, our own Christian community, our own roots, that has particular relevance to present-day concerns, especially in a time of rootlessness and preoccupation with the privatistic and the individualistic.

Building on the basis of an historical perspective rooted in the Lutheran tradition, and of a knowledge of where it has been and how it got there, Lutheran hymnody in America can build on its impressive accomplishments, avoid the repetition of past mistakes, and move toward the future, solidly grounded in the spirit and the content of Lutheranism's beginnings in the 16th century. Only in this way will the completeness of Muhlenberg's vision—whatever shape it may take in the years ahead—become a reality. Only in this way will Lutheranism in America find its way beyond the mere appearance of a common hymnody to one that captures both the spirit and the substance of Lutheranism's unique contribution to the church's song.

1

The Background
of the 16th-Century
Lutheran Reformation

A significant contribution of the Lutheran Reformation to the church catholic was the prominence it gave to matter of congregational song. "The sudden bursting forth of the Lutheran chorale," notes Ulrich Leupold, "is one of the most thrilling chapters in the history of the Reformation."[1] Bard Thompson suggests that one of the three most significant contributions of the Reformation church was the restoration of song to the people.[2]

While the singing of popular religious hymns and songs was not unknown in the Middle Ages, its occurrence in connection with the liturgy was infrequent, sporadic, and—except in certain circumstances—proscribed by the church. The tradition of singing by the people was, however, kept alive in a variety of ways: through the singing of *Leisen* (songs in which each stanza concluded with some form of "Kyrie eleison"), popular songs in the Meistersinger and Minnesinger traditions, songs of the Flagellants and other enthusiasts of the 13th and 14th centuries, the songs produced by the mystics of the 14th century, as well as the general movement toward the vernacular that was evident already in the centuries before the Reformation. It remained for Luther to give the movement toward vernacular religious song not only a common, universal thrust, but, more importantly, a focus in the liturgy that was to become a distinguishing mark of Reformation song.

Luther's concern for vernacular congregational song was not simply a concern that the people had something to sing. Rather he saw the Lutheran chorale as a vehicle for the people's singing of the liturgy. Most of the chorales that emerged in the early years of the Reformation had a particular focus in the liturgy, whether they were strophic settings of parts of the Ordinary of the Mass (Kyrie, Gloria, Credo, Sanctus, or Agnus Dei hymns), paraphrases of psalms, de tempore hymns, baptismal or eucharistic hymns, or those chorales related to specific seasons and festivals of the church year.

Moreover, the Reformation chorale was, for Luther and his followers, a vehicle for doxological proclamation. The function of the chorale was proclamatory, telling the story of salvation; it was to "proclaim the wonders God has done." The chorale was a confession of faith, not a vehicle for personal feelings or emotion. It was designed neither to be listened to, nor as a vehicle for entertainment. It was meant to be sung by a congregation as a vehicle through which they professed their common faith, rehearsed the story of salvation, and proclaimed God's Word to the world. The essential concept of the chorale as it developed in the Lutheran Reformation was that it was "the biblical word itself, not its substitute; it [was] an essential part of the liturgy, not its appendage."[3]

This was the essence of the Lutheran Reformation chorale: doxological proclamation with its focus in the liturgy. As such the hymn or the hymnal was a confessional writing in a special sense of the word, and the singing of the chorale was in reality a confessional act. One has only to look at the hymns and the hymn collections of 16th-century Lutheranism to see these ideas carried out with clarity and precision.

As early as his Latin Mass of 1523, Luther expressed the wish that "we had as many songs as possible in the vernacular which the people could sing during mass."[4] Toward the end of 1523 Luther wrote to George Spalatin asking for his help in writing new vernacular hymn texts based on the psalms.[5] Luther himself wrote a number of hymn texts which, together with some by his friends, were printed as broadsheets—single leaflets—and found wide acceptance.[6] The decades following the Reformation demonstrate how Luther's concern worked its way out in the unprecedented flowering of congregational song in those places where Lutheranism took root.

The oldest Lutheran hymn collection appeared in 1524 as *Etlich Cristlich lider*, a compilation of eight texts—four by Luther, three by Paul Speratus, one by an unnamed author—with five tunes. Published in Wittenberg by Jobst Gutknecht of Nuernberg, it was undoubtedly a compilation from earlier broadsheets and appeared in three editions in 1524 and is usually known as the *Achtliederbuch* (The Book of Eight Hymns). The title, which indicates that the contents of the collection was to be used "to sing in church as it is in part already practiced in Wittenberg,"[7] suggests that Luther had already begun to introduce congregational singing in the Wittenberg church as early as 1523. Each succeeding year saw the publication of additional hymn collections. Among the cities that vied to produce better and more comprehensive collections were Magdeburg, Zwickau, Leipzig, Erfurt, Nuernberg, Augsburg, and Königsberg.[8] Some of the more important collections of the next half-century are the following:

1524
Etlich Cristlich lider. Published in Wittenberg. 8 texts, 5 tunes. Published by Jobst Gutknecht.
Enchiridion oder Handbuechlein. Published in Erfurt "zeum schwartzenn Horne bey der Kremer Brucken" by Mattheus Maler, 25 texts, 15 tunes.
Enchiridion oder Handbuchlein. Published in Erfurt "yn der Permenter Gassen zum Ferbefasz" by Ludwig Trutebul. Same as the above.

1525
Reprints of the Erfurt *Enchiridion* in Erfurt, Zwickau, Breslau, Nuernberg, Straszburg.

Teutsch Kirchenampt mit lobgesengen und goettlichen Psalmen wie es die gemein zu Straszburg singt.

1526
Enchiridion geystlicher gesenge und Psalmen. Printed at Wittenberg by Michael Lotther. 42 texts with melodies.
Psalmen, gebett und Kirchenuebung, wie sie zu Straszburg gehalten werden. 21 melodies.

1529
Geistliche Lieder aufs neue gebessert zu Wittenberg. Martin Luther. Reprints appeared in 1531 in Wittenberg, Erfurt, Rostock.

1530
Enchiridion geistliche Gesaenge und Psalmen. Printed in Leipzig by Michael Blum. 63 texts, 27 tunes.

1535
Das Wittenberger Gesangbuch. Published by Joseph Klug. Probably the 2nd edition of Klug's book of 1529 containing 52 texts, 53 tunes, the Litany, Te Deum, and 20 canticles from the Old and New Testaments.

1539
Geistliche lieder auffs new gebessert und gemehrt zu Wittenberg. D. Martinus Luther. Published in Leipzig by Valten Schumann.

1542
Christliche Geseng, Lateinisch und Deutsch, zum Begrebnis. D. Martinus Luther. Published by Joseph Klug, 12 Latin, 6 German burial hymns. Luther put new texts to the old melodies saying: "The melodies and notes are precious. It would be a pity to let them perish."

1545
Geistliche Lieder. Published in Leipzig by Valentin Babst, 89 hymns plus 40 in an Appendix, with melodies.

1569
Kirchengesaenge. Frankfurt am Main. A hymnal in folio for

24

pastors, schoolmasters, and cantors, 380 hymns, 223 melodies.

1573

Kirchengesaenge. A Collection from the best hymn books and agendas by Johannes Keuchenthal, containing liturgical music, 200 congregational hymns, 165 melodies.

Of the more than 200 hymn collections of various sizes published between 1525–1575 in connection with the Lutheran Reformation,[9] one stands out above all the others. This is the *Geistliche Lieder* of 1545 published in Leipzig by Valentin Babst; the so-called Babst hymnal.[10] One early 20th-century church music historian called the Babst hymnal "the most significant hymnal of the 16th century."[11] Ulrich Leupold's evaluation describes it as "the finest hymnal of the Reformation period,"[12] and "the most complete and carefully edited hymnal to appear in Luther's lifetime."[13] The book contains numerous illustrations, and each page was illustrated and bordered with elaborate designs.

The Babst hymnal was important for a number of reasons. By the time of its publication, slightly more than a quarter century after the beginning of the Reformation, the number of hymns it contained—89 texts plus 40 additional texts in an Appendix, virtually each text with its own melody—had grown appreciably since the earliest collections and was a significantly more mature collection than the earlier, smaller fascicles. It was also important because its content was widely representative of the various musical sources from which the Lutheran chorale had sprung: the chants of the Catholic church, the pre-Reformation Leisen, well-known non-liturgical pre-Reformation songs, contrafacta, and newly written hymns. It was also specifically endorsed by Martin Luther who wrote the Preface, the last such Preface he would write before his death the year following the publication of the Babst hymnbook.[14] In the selection of its hymns and in its arrangement—according to the church year—the Babst hymnal represented the maturing view of the 16th-century Reformation church's understanding of the role of congregational hymnody. The Babst hymnbook began with a warning of Luther that was not entirely unjustified.

> Many false masters now hymns indite.
> Be on your guard and judge them aright.
> Where God is building his church and word,
> There comes the devil with lie and sword.[15]

Soon after Luther's death new and different kinds of hymn collections began to appear. Some were limited to versifications of the Psalter or the Gospels and Epistles, while others were planned, according to Blume, along "lines that the Reformer certainly would not have approved."[16]

As to its hymnic content, the Babst hymnal reflected the most significant and representative consensus regarding a Reformation "core" of evangelical hymnody (*Kernlieder*) that the 16th century produced and which was considered normative for Lutheran congregational song through the middle of the 17th century.[17]

This collection of Reformation hymnody spread like wildfire throughout those parts of the European continent where the Lutheran Reformation took hold. The new song of the Reformation was promoted and furthered through the efforts of many of both high and low estate. Students from the Scandinavian countries, for example, who had come to Wittenberg to study, took the chorales back with them to their homeland.

The first hymnal specifically prepared for Lutheran use in Denmark, Hans Thomisson's *Den danske Psalme-bog* of 1569, contained a number of translations from earlier German collections. Melodies that Thomisson borrowed from German collections included *Nun komm der Heiden Heiland*, and *Christum wir sollen loben schon*, both tunes based on earlier Gregorian chants. Four years later, Nils Jesperson's *Gradual* (1573) included Danish translations with melodies of the German texts "Aus tiefer Not," "Christ lag in Todesbanden," "Isaiah dem Propheten," and "Ein feste Burg." This collection also included such melodies as *Guds Lam Wskyldig* (Lamb of God, pure and holy) and *J Tro Allesammen Paa En Gud* (We all believe in one true God).[18]

The earliest Swedish hymnals liberally used various chorales from a variety of German hymn books. When Gustaf I ascended the Swedish throne in 1523, Liemohn notes that he "advanced the cause of the Reformation in Sweden, [and] accepted the church folk song introduced by Luther although changed from its original rhythm. The chorales were in this form accepted for the Swedish service."[19] Even as late as the end of the 17th century, the hymnic heritage of the Reformation persisted in use in Sweden. The *Swenska Psalmboken* of 1695 was the first such book to be officially authorized and its use required in all churches. In the music edition of this collection of 1695, Harold Vallerius' *Koralpsalmboken* of 1697, the preservation of the old traditions in church music was still clearly evident. "Here," according to Joel Lundeen, "are found the great Reformation chorales in their original rhythmic and modal forms together with Swedish tunes and those inherited from the plainsong period."[20]

In England, Miles Coverdale's *Goostly Psalmes and Spiritualle Songes* [21](c. 1539) is another example of how the Lutheran chorale was spreading throughout the countries associated in one way or another with the Reformation. This collection of 41 hymns and metrical psalms contained 13 metrical psalms, metrical versions of the Magnificat, Nunc Dimittis, the Lord's Prayer, Creed, the Ten Commandments, and a number of Latin and German hymns, including many of Luther's texts. Among the translations of Luther's hymn texts are his Nicene Creed ("Wir glauben all"), both versions of his Ten Commandments hymns ("Dies sind die heiligen zehn Gebot" and "Mensch willst du leben seliglich"), "Nun freut euch lieben Christen gemein," and "Es ist da Heil uns kommen her." The words and music of this collection were "largely Lutheran in origin."[22] The music "drew largely on Gregorian chant and German chorales and all settings were in unison."[23] That Coverdale's work was banned before it could even begin to take hold—being listed in a catalog of forbidden books in the Injunction issued by King Henry VIII in 1539—was one of the ironies in the history of the

Reformation chorale. One wonders what the later history of the chorale in England might have been had the king not taken this action.

In one form or another, many of the early Reformation chorales found their way into congregational song wherever Lutheranism flourished. That they did so is a tribute to their vital, Gospel-centered texts and the vigorous melodies with which those texts were associated. The texts were confessional, proclamatory, songs of thanks and praise. That these texts were associated with tunes derived from a rich variety of sources made them accessible, broadly appealing, and singable. While in their origin many of these tunes sprang from German soil, they were melodies that were international in style and universal in substance, having developed from such diverse influences as Gregorian chant, common ballads, pre-Reformation popular songs, as well as newly composed tunes. When translated into the local vernacular and sung by the people—whether in German, Danish, Swedish, English, or Norwegian—they were *Lutheran* chorales ex-pressive of the Reformation faith whose specific geographical provenance was largely immaterial.

The following centuries saw a number of important changes in the 16th-century chorale. Part of the story developed in these pages is the attempt to answer the question, What happened to that normative core of Lutheran congregational song in the succession of Lutheran hymnbooks that followed the Reformation period? This is also an important part of the story of Lutheran hymnbooks in America. Both Pietism and a rationalism born of the Enlightenment wreaked their own particular textual and musical havoc on the chorale. And with the development of a growing sense of national consciousness in the Scandinavian countries in the 19th century and an accompanying blossoming of a native hymnody, the Reformation chorales began to wane in popularity and were seen by some as "foreign" elements.

These hymns and chorales, or at least some of them, were among the texts and tunes the earliest Lutheran settlers in

North America brought with them as they came to the New World in the latter 17th and early 18th centuries. They were the "people's song" whose texts uniquely expressed the theological insights of the Reformation regarding music as proclamation and praise, and presented in music that reflected the honesty, directness, and vitality of those texts.

In the two and one-half centuries following the Reformation, the confessional hymnody of Reformation Lutheranism was significantly affected—both on the Continent and in America—by Pietism and, later, rationalism. Pietism sought to give a larger place to individual experience and human feelings and, in hymnody, often led to extreme subjectivism, sentimentalism, and other deleterious results. Rationalism, which sought to bring hymnody in line with human reason, had equally devastating consequences. How this all worked its way out in the hymnody of the Lutherans who began to come to the New World less than one hundred years after the first Lutheran hymn collection of 1524 and less than 75 years after the publication of the Babst hymnal of 1545 is the story to which we now turn.

2

Early Evidence of Lutheran Hymnody in North America

The earliest hints and suggestions of Lutheran hymnody in North America are to be found in the early expeditions from Denmark, Holland, and Sweden in the 17th century. Some of these settlements—particularly that of the Danes—were sporadic and transitory, lasting perhaps a year at best. The Dutch and the Swedes, by contrast, established settlements that were to last a good bit longer. These are the earliest beginnings of the story of Lutheran hymnody in America. While the facts of their settlements are quite clear, the matter of their hymnody is not at all clear in the early documents. What is certain, however, is that Lutherans have, from the beginning, sung their faith. It would have been quite unusual had not these early settlers done the same.

The Danes on Hudson Bay

Perhaps the earliest evidence of Lutherans in the New World is that of the Jens Munck expedition, authorized by Christian IV of Denmark. It sailed west from Denmark in 1619 with two ships, 66 men, and the hope of finding a northern route to East India.[1] Touching the southern coast of Greenland in July 1619, and sailing north of New-foundland through the Labrador Sea, they entered Hudson's Bay and arrived at its western shore near the Churchill River and established a settlement they called "Nova Dania" (New

Denmark), a year before the "Mayflower" sailed from England bringing the earliest English settlers to the New World.

There was a pastor with the group, Rasmus Jensen, and presumably hymns were sung as part of the services he conducted. They would likely have been taken from Hans Thomisson's *Den danske Psalmebog* (1569), the first hymnal specifically prepared for the Lutheran service in Denmark, published just 50 years prior to this expedition. It contained a number of translations from the earlier German collections together with their melodies. Other possible sources of hymns could have been such earlier collections as Claus Mortensen's *Det kristelige Messeembede*(1528) which contained some hymns, or the Malmo *Salmebogen* (c. 1531), which became the hymnal generally used by the evangelical church in Denmark until it was replaced by Hans Tausen's hymnal in 1544.

The Danish settlement was short-lived. Most of the settlers, including the Danish pastor who accompanied the group, died within the year, only two sailors and Munck himself managing to return safely to their homeland. If the members of this expedition sang hymns, as they most probably did, we can say that this band of hardy sailors from Denmark was the first to sing Lutheran hymns in North America. The sounds of their hymns, however, were as short-lived as the settlement.

The Dutch in Ft. Orange and New York

It should not be surprising that when the Dutch West India Company sent settlers to the New World there should be some Lutherans among them,[2] for in the early 1600s strong Lutheran congregations existed in such cities as Amsterdam, Rotterdam, and Leyden. In 1623 a shipload of settlers from the Dutch West India Company reached America, the largest group consisting of 18 families who settled at Ft. Orange near the city of Albany. Just two years later, in 1625, 45 persons from Holland settled on Manhattan

Island and founded New Amsterdam. Lutherans found the practice of their faith in New Amsterdam somewhat difficult under the official religion of the colony, which was that of the Reformed Church. The following description illuminates their problems.

When the Lutherans in New Amsterdam [New York City] and Fort Orange [Albany] banded together in 1649 as a congregation designated as the Lutheran Church in the colony of Netherland, there appeared to be every prospect of a strong and flourishing church. But the colony was in the hands of the Dutch, whose official religion was Calvinistic (or Reformed). So far as the Dutch authorities were concerned there was room for only one religion, and that was their own. When some Lutheran laymen in the colony began holding services, they were fined and threatened with heavier fines if they repeated the offense. Then when the Amsterdam Lutheran Church in 1657 sent a young Lutheran pastor, Johannes Ernestus Gutwasser, to New Amsterdam, a storm broke loose. Gutwasser was summarily ordered to leave the colony. He went into hiding on Long Island but was eventually arrested and deported in 1659. The strictest watch was kept everywhere and only a few services were held during Gutwasser's brief period of freedom. None at all were held, so far as is known, after he was deported. That definitely crushed the Lutheran movement for the duration of the Dutch period.[3]

It was not until the English conquered New Amsterdam in 1664, renaming it New York, that greater religious freedom was extended to its inhabitants. In 1669 the church in Holland sent Jacob Fabritius to serve as pastor to the Lutherans. He restored the traditional Lutheran hymnody and liturgy as it was practiced in Holland. Several pastors followed Fabritius, among them Bernhard Arnzius and Andrew Rudman who—in 1703, in what was probably the first regular ordination in the New World, representing the archbishop of Uppsala in a full Latin service with choir at "Old Swedes Church" in Philadelphia—ordained Justus Falkner to be his successor to serve the Dutch congregations in New York. Falckner's successor was William Berkenmeyer who continued his ministry until his death in 1751, just eight years after Heinrich Melchior Muhlenberg had begun his ministry in Pennsylvania.

Throughout this period there are frequent comments about the lack of hymnals in the New World and repeated requests to the Amsterdam Consistory to send hymnals, but they seem to have gone unanswered. Minutes of the Consistory of July 6, 1712 resolved "to send to [Pastor Falckner] and to donate to the aforesaid congregation one large folio Bible, 50 Psalters, 50 *Paradijshofjens* (Paradise Gardens), and 50 Haverman's prayer books."[4] This mention of the *Paradijshofjens* (Paradise Gardens) is the first hymnal of which we have a specific mention. However, there is no description of its contents nor any further information, despite several references to this collection in the correspondence between Pastor Falckner and the Consistory in Amsterdam. In addition to the mention of the *Paradijshofjens* there is a brief mention in the Consistory Minutes of February 4, 1754 of a request that copies of the Marburg hymnal, a German hymnal that was in great favor among the Germans in Pennsylvania, be sent to the church in New York.[5] Apparently none were available. The frequent lament was that, among other things, "we lack suitable hymnals." It would be a common complaint in the decades ahead.

The Swedes on the Delaware

In 1638 Lutherans from Sweden sailed up the Delaware River in two ships and established a settlement near present-day Wilmington, Delaware, and called it New Sweden. Here they built Fort Christina, two houses, and Holy Trinity ("Old Swedes") Church. Peter Minuit, the former director-general for the Dutch in New Amsterdam, was partly responsible for this new colony. Having been dismissed from New Amsterdam, he went to Sweden where he sought to create interest in a Swedish colony along the Delaware River. This expedition was the result.[6]

A second group arrived in 1640 with Reorus Torkillus, a

pastor who served the colonists at Fort Christina where a temporary chapel was erected. A second pastor, John Campanius, arrived a year later and joined the second group of colonists at Tinicum Island, nine miles southwest of present-day Philadelphia. Campanius is noted especially for his work with the Indians, into whose language he translated Luther's Small Catechism. Despite conflicts with the Dutch and the resulting return of many of the colonists to Sweden, the Swedish Lutheran Church remained a presence here until 1831 when the last of its missionaries, Nicholas Collin, died. Most of the Swedes then affiliated with the Episcopal Church.

Amandus Johnson, describing the worship of these colonists, says the following:

> The Swedish order of service was followed in the colony. Printz writes in 1644 that "the services with its ceremonies are conducted as in old Sweden" and in the "good old Swedish language." "Our priest," he says, "is vested with a chasuble and differs in all manner from the other sects surrounding us." The order of services at "High Mass," as given in the Psalm-book of 1614 which was used here (1640–97) was as follows: . . .[7]

The service of the Psalm-book of 1614 followed this order:

An allocution
Confession of sins
Singing of the Kyrie and Gloria in excelsis (Instead of the Laudamus, Decius' setting of the Gloria may be sub-stituted)
Salutation (with the congregation singing the response, and followed by the appropriate collects)
The Epistle and the Gospel (between which there was an appropriate Swedish hymn)
Either the Apostles' or the Nicene Creed, or Luther's setting of the Creed
Sermon, preceded by a hymn
Salutation, prefaces, and the Consecration, followed by reading or singing the Sanctus. The celebrant then sings the

Lord's Prayer followed by the Admonition
Distribution of the Elements during the congregational singing
    of the Agnus Dei
Various closing sentences, concluding with the Benediction
Final hymn

The frequent use of hymnody in this order is evident. It clearly shows the continuation of the Reformation practice of substituting appropriate congregational hymns for parts of the Ordinary of the Mass,[8] the use of the de tempore practice in the hymn between the Epistle and Gospel, as well as other uses of hymnody in the service. One can only view with admiration the determination of these immigrants to sing the songs of faith in the New World as they had in the old.

The Swedes maintained close connection with the church in their homeland. When the Swedish government in 1696 sent pastors Andrew Rudman and Eric Bjorck to serve the settlers, they brought with them 50 copies of the Uppsala hymnbook and 100 other hymn books together with Bibles and other devotional material. In 1704 King Charles XII provided a second shipment of 400 hymnbooks in quarto as well as 300 other hymnbooks. In 1712 when pastors Hesselius and Lidenius came to serve the Swedish churches, they brought along 360 copies of Svedberg's edition of the hymnal in a variety of sizes. Such shipments of books from the homeland—Wolf notes 500 additional copies of Svedberg's hymnal sent in 1721, 24 new psalmbooks brought in 1747, and 50 psalmbooks brought in 1750—continued until about the middle of the 18th century when English gradually began to replace Swedish as the official language in the churches.[9]

The contribution of the early Swedish Lutheran settlers are many. Among them is their upholding of the liturgical tradition of their homeland at a time and in a place where most American denominations restricted their music and their singing to metrical psalmody. Wolf cites their "extensive use of hymnbooks, their intonations of liturgical texts such as the collects, and their early introduction of organ support for the services"[10] as evidence of their importance. As a rising tide of German immigrants in the first half of the 18th century began to eclipse the Swedish settlements, they nevertheless provided a model for the German Lutherans when they first began to organize congregations. It is to the story of the German immigrants that we now turn.

3

The First Lutheran Hymnbook and Chorale Book in America

The great tide of Lutheran immigrants into colonial America came from Germany, not Sweden, and occurred in the first half of the 18th century.[1] This great immigration began in the early decades of the 1700s when many Germans from the Palatinate moved up the Hudson River in 1708-10 and established both Lutheran and Reformed churches as far north as the Mohawk River. By the middle 1700s, there were 26 Lutheran congregations in New York and 19 in New Jersey.

In Pennsylvania, however, the number of German immigrants grew at an astounding rate. In 1730 at least 21 Lutheran congregations were established in Pennsylvania. By 1750 the Lutheran population had grown to more than 60,000 in Pennsylvania alone. While the Lutherans who settled in South Carolina and Georgia tended to come directly from Europe, much of the Lutheran presence in such places as Delaware, Maryland, Virginia, West Virginia, and North Carolina arrived there via Pennsylvania. This dramatic increase in the Lutheran population in North America presented both problems as well as challenges—not only for the settlers themselves, but for the Lutheran churches in Germany upon whom the settlers were dependent for a continuing supply of pastors.

German Pietism and Hymnody

The hymnody with which these German Lutheran immigrants to America in the century preceding the Revolutionary War were acquainted—and which formed an important part of their piety—was shaped and molded to a large extent by German Pietism of the late 17th and early 18th centuries.[2] Pietism, a movement that developed largely as a reaction against what its adherents perceived to be a sterile and intellectualized orthodoxy, is largely associated with the names of Philipp Jacob Spener (1635–1705) and August Hermann Francke (1663–1727). Spener's book *Pia desideria* (1675) contained his attack on the established church and his recommendations for restoring spiritual life to what he considered a sterile and formalized church. Francke established a center for the movement of Pietism at the University of Halle, to which he went in 1698, and especially emphasized the need for mission work. Pietism, reacting against a congregational life which it characterized as cold and formal, emphasized a practical and deeply personal piety. It sought to restore a more vigorous spiritual life by emphasizing personal Bible study, prayer, and works of Christian charity.

The hymnody of Pietism also reflected this new emphasis that marked a decided change from the hymnody of the early Reformation.[3] The transition from a churchly, confessional hymnody to hymns of a more pietistic and devotional character—from *Bekenntnisslieder* (confessional hymns) to *Erbauungslieder* (devotional hymns)—was already evident in the Lutheran hymn writers of the last half of the 17th century. The hymns of Paul Gerhardt (1607–76), Johann Franck (1618–77), Johann Rist (1607–73), Georg Neumark (1621–81), Michael Schirmer (1606–73), and Johann Scheffler (1624–77) reflected the beginnings of this transition. While the hymn writers of this time were, for the most part, orthodox, they added a fervent piety and a mystic quality that had not characterized earlier Lutheran hymnody. By the early years of the 18th century, characterized by Wilhelm Nelle as the "summer of pietistic hymnody,"[4] a mighty river of hymnody was surging forth reflecting every shade of Christian experience. At its best, Pietism was rich with the fullness of devotional fervor and made significant contributions to the church's song. At its worst, it often degenerated into irreverent sentimentalism.

Both textually and musically, Pietism's hymnody stood in stark contrast to the hymnody of the early Reformation. In pietistic circles "nothing was encouraged but 'spiritual songs' of the narrowest type, which followed the verse as closely and simply as possible."[5] The vigorous rhythmic melodies of the 16th century were gradually abandoned and replaced by a new kind of melody in which the tune proceeded in even-note fashion. Liemohn characterizes this change in the following way.

> The spirit of subjectivism which characterized the Pietistic movement deserted the rugged, forceful melodies of the Reformation and used instead a freer-moving Italian operatic type of melody. . . . The use of triple meter became common, often resulting in a waltz-like movement. . . . The more staid German music was now subjected to the rapidly spreading ornamental Italian music of the period which was considered more "artistic" than the German.[6]

Friedrich Blume concludes that the large outpouring of Pietistic hymnody resulted in a reduction in the number of traditional Lutheran hymns available in 18th-century hymnbooks, as well as decreasing the general worth of the poetry and music in such books. "The more Pietistic a hymnbook was," he says, "the more its traditional stock of hymns was crushed, modernized, and rationalized,"[7] and "the more Pietistic a hymn book's origin and author, the less noteworthy was the music."[8] The new hymnody of Pietism spread rapidly, the new gaining favor often at the expense of the old.

Among the important hymnals from this period were the *Geistreiches Gesangbuch*[9] (1704) published in Halle and edited by Johann Anastasii Freylinghausen and his Neues

Geistreiches Gesangbuch[10](1714), also printed in Halle. These two books, subsequently bound together and reissued as one book in 1741[11] and again 30 years later in 1771,[12] containing 1581 hymns with 597 melodies, were frequently referred to as the "Freylinghausen Gesangbuch" or the "Halle hymnal" (after the Halle Orphanage which published and distributed it throughout Germany). The music in the hymnal consisted of melody with figured bass. The influence of this book extended to America through the many immigrants who brought with them one or another version of the "Halle hymnal." Among these was Henry Melchior Muhlenberg himself, who had been given a copy of this book by the wife of August Hermann Francke on the day of his ordination.[13] The "Halle" or "Freylinghausen" hymnal was to exert a considerable influence on the first "made in America" Lutheran hymnal. It is significant that Frey-linghausen's *Geistreiches Gesangbuch* of 1741, perhaps the most influential hymnal of Pietism, still retained the historic *Kernlieder* of the 16th-century Reformation.

Other pietistic hymnals that were popular in Germany and that found their way to America were the hymnals of Marburg, Wuerttemberg, Wernergirode, and Coethen. These hymnals were interdependent and mutually reinforcing; but it was the Halle hymnal that remained the touchstone of Pietism's hymnody in Germany. Its influence in determining the shape of early German Lutheran hymnody in America was to be equally decisive.

Muhlenberg and the *Erbauliche Liedersammlung* of 1786

It was Gotthilf August Francke (1696–1769), son of August Hermann Francke—a leading German pietist and ardent disciple of Philipp Spener, the "Father of Pietism"—who persuaded Heinrich Melchior Muhlenberg, in September of 1741, to accept a call to the "United Lutheran Congregations" in Pennsylvania.[14] The number of German Lutheran immigrants to the New World was dramatically increasing. This startling increase and the accompanying need for pastors and funding for this mission land far outstripped the resources of the church in Germany. The repeated requests for help from the German Lutheran immigrants in America had become more urgent with the presence of Count Nicholas von Zinzendorf in the American colonies who "appeared in Pennsylvania posing as a Lutheran holding inter-denominational conferences, and assuming leadership among the shepherdless Lutherans of the colony."[15] The authorities at Halle, finally goaded into action, felt they had found in Muhlenberg the person who had the skill, temperament, and ability to address the problems of the Lutherans in America and help the church begin the move from the status of mission church to an independent and self-reliant Lutheran Church in America.

Born in Einbeck, Germany, Muhlenberg (1711–87) had received his theological training at the University of Goettingen and for 15 months had taught at the Halle Orphanage. Ordained in 1739, he was knowledgeable in languages and music and had thought for a time of going to India as a missionary. He was persuaded, however, to accept a position at a country church in Grosshennersdorf in Saxony where he served as diaconus and inspector of an orphans' home 1739–41. On a visit to Halle in September of 1741, he met Francke who urged him to consider going to America, a call which he promptly accepted. Arriving unannounced in Philadelphia on November 25, 1742, after having spent a week among the Salzburg Lutherans in South Carolina, he found his flock confused, disorganized, and in disarray. Within just a short time, however, he was able to establish himself, was ordained on December 27, 1742 in Gloria Dei Church, Philadelphia, by Peter Tranberg, the Swedish pastor at Wilmington, Delaware, and the three churches—known as the "United Congregations": the churches at Philadelphia, New Providence (now Trappe), and New Hanover (Falkner's Swamp)—welcomed him as their pastor.

GOD'S SONG IN A NEW LAND

Muhlenberg was a staunch Lutheran, loyal to the Lutheran Confessions. His Lutheranism, however, was influenced by the pietistic spirit of the times, a factor strengthened by his friendship with Francke and his association with the Halle Orphanage where he taught for a year following his graduation from the university.[16]

On his arrival in America, Muhlenberg was confronted by the same variety of hymnals which had been so evident in Germany. The Marburg hymnal was widely used in Pennsylvania and throughout the colonies[17] and was reprinted as late as the end of the 18th century. In other places the so-called "Coethen Songs,"[18] the Wuerttemberg hymnal of 1741,[19] and the Wernigerode hymnbook[20] were in use. The Halle hymnal, however, was undoubtedly the most widely known and used.[21] Muhlenberg's journals are replete with references to the Halle hymns and indicate that they were well known and used in many places in the German Lutheran settlements.[22] Muhlenberg noted the use of the Halle hymnbook on board ship during his voyage to America.

[On board the ship on the way to America] I refreshed them [the Salzburgers] also with a few physical benefits, and especially with a number of hymns from the new Halle hymnbook which had been presented to me by the worthy wife of Dr. Francke on the day of my vocation.[23]

However, one of the most poignant references to the place which these hymns held in the daily life of Muhlenberg's family is the description of the death of his young son. The entry dated February 16, 1764 is as follows:

All afternoon until evening we had a steady stream of friends who came to visit because of our sick child . . . When we sang several stanzas of the powerful Halle hymns for him, he expressed his sorrow that he could not sing with us, but showed his joy nevertheless. Near ten o'clock, when I had put him on my lap for the last time and was about to put him back in bed, he lovingly kissed me good-by, and after both his parents had sung the hymn,

"Breit aus die Fluegel beide, O Jesu, meine Freude," etc. he fell
quietly asleep in this Redeemer upon whose all-holy merit he had
been baptized.[24]

By 1748, through faithful preaching and pastoral work,
Muhlenberg had organized the Ministerium of Pennsylvania, the first Lutheran synod in the United States. The
matter of a hymnal to unite the scattered German Lutheran
throughout the colonies, as important as it apparently was to
Muhlenberg, was forced to wait upon more urgent matters.

It was not until 38 years after the formation of the
Pennsylvania Ministerium that action was set in motion to
correct this situation. On the afternoon of June 4, 1782 the
35th convention of the Evangelical Lutheran Minis-terium
in North America meeting in Lancaster, Pennsyl-vania,
unanimously resolved "to have a new Hymn Book printed
for our United Congregations."[25] The details of the
resolution appointed a committee consisting of the Revs.
Muhlenberg, Sr., John Christopher Kunze, J. H. C. Helmuth,
and Muhlenberg, Jr. to prepare the book and noted that the
committee be strictly bound by the following rules:

1. As far as possible to follow the arrangement of the Halle
   Hymn Book.
2. Not to omit any of the old standard hymns, especially of
   Luther and Paul Gerhard[t].
3. To omit the Gospels and Epistles for Apostles' Day, Minor
   Festivals, and the History of the Destruction of Jerusalem,
   together with the collection of Prayers and the Catechism.
4. To report all this together with incidental changes, e.g., the
   Litany to a special meeting of Synod.
5. Not to admit more than 750 hymns into the collection.[26]

It was also noted that the Senior Muhlenberg was to prepare
the Preface and that it be signed by all the United Preachers.
By August of that same year Muhlenberg noted that he had
"gathered together some materials, since at the end of the
synod meeting the task of preparing a preface to the proposed
hymnbook was assigned to me."[27] However, it was not until
January of 1783 that Muhlenberg's work on the hymnal

began in earnest.

While the exact division of labor among the members of the committee is difficult to determine, it is clear that in the early stages of the work Muhlenberg played a most significant role. In shaping a hymnal for the German Lutherans in America, Muhlenberg, while retaining a strong confessional concern, drew from the sources that were at hand and with which he was acquainted. These sources were the hymnals and hymnody of Pietism. He notes on January 15, 1783 that

> I began to write the preface to the hymnbook, which has been assigned to me, in somewhat altered and shortened form. Now I shall also have to spend several days selecting the hymns which are to be included in the new hymnbook.

In less than a week the bulk of the hymns had apparently been selected and he devoted his energies to the task of indexing them. His entry for January 21, 1783 provides additional information.

1. The Reverend Ministerial Conference decided upon seven hundred and fifty hymns for the new hymnbook.
2. I have underlined five hundred and thirty-four according to the rubrics in the Halle selection; therefore, two hundred and sixteen of the required number are lacking.
3. There may be many powerful and Spirit-filled hymns in the large Halle, Wernigerode, Coethen, etc. hymnbooks which would fill out the number, but I do not have these books. My esteemed brethren will be kind enough to criticize and improve my selection, to subtract from it or add to it.[28]

Particularly interesting are Muhlenberg's comments on how he handled certain details of his editorial ask.

> Those hymns which expect the last judgment of the world in the too-near future and mention the signs that precede it I have left out. I also have not included those which, inspired by the Song of Solomon, are composed too close to the verge of sensuality, and also those that dally with diminutives—for example, "little Jesus," "little brother," "little angels," etc.

These appear to me to be too childish and not in accord with Scripture, even though they were intended to be childlike and familiar. The ancient and medieval hymns, which have been familiar to all Lutherans from childhood on, cannot well be left out; even though they sound somewhat harsh in construction, rhyme, etc., they are nevertheless orthodox.[29]

Thus the Halle hymnbook provided both the pattern for the arrangement of the hymnal as well as the source for the bulk of the hymnody itself.[30] The Ministerium meeting in York, Pennsylvania in June 1784 resolved to print 1,000 copies of the book, that the account of the Destruction of Jerusalem and Luther's Catechism remain without additions, that the Litany be transferred to the Prayer Book, and that the Preface prepared by the Senior Muhlenberg be printed unchanged, except for a slight addition from Pliny regarding the hymns of the early Christians.[31]

The time it took for the hymnal to appear in printed form was hardly equal to the speed with which it had been compiled. There were problems with the printer, and a committee addressed the problems of shortening and altering some of the hymns. By February 1786 Helmuth noted that "almost four hundred hymns have been printed"[32] and asked that Muhlenberg send him the Preface which he did later that month. On October 20, 1786 Muhlenberg received from Helmuth a copy of the portrait of Martin Luther which was to be used as the frontispiece for the hymnal.[33] Sometime later that fall the hymnal appeared as the *Erbauliche Liedersammlung zum Gottesdienstlichen Gebrauch in den Vereinigten Evangelisch Lutherischen Gemeinen in Nord-America*,[34] the first German Lutheran hymnbook to be made and published in America, containing 706 hymns.

By making available a single hymnal that could serve the scattered Lutheran communities, Muhlenberg was thus taking the first step toward what he hoped would be a truly "common hymnbook." His concern was expressed and summarized in his Preface to the *Erbauliche Liedersammlung*.

We should note what until now has hindered complete unity in connection with singing in our public worship, namely the many kinds of hymnbooks, since in almost every one various little alterations have been made, and in some there are few hymns, in others many. *If only there were one hymnbook for all American congregations which would contain the best of the old and new spiritual songs, how much more convenient and harmonious it would be.* And why should the evangelical congregations not have the authority and right to introduce their own hymnbook, as long as they still enjoy the priceless freedom of religion and conscience? What matters is not the number of hymns, but rather the choice of the best and most powerful, and for that we still have—thank God—freedom and opportunity, as sensible and experienced Christians can themselves perceive from this book.[35] [Emphasis mine]

Muhlenberg's *Erbauliche Liedersammlung* was a hymnal born in the period of pietism which, nevertheless, still retained a healthy concern for orthodoxy. It made significant provision for the church year, and breathed a warm and churchly spirit. Some 64 years after its appearance as conservative a journal as *Der Lutheraner*, edited by C. F. W. Walther of the Evangelical Lutheran Synod of Missouri, Ohio, and Other States, could speak of it with high praise.[36] "It was an excellent book and contained all of the old solid hymns, especially those of Luther and Gerhard, unaltered,"[37] remarked John Nicum, prominent Lutheran church historian at the end of the following century.

In the years following its appearance minor revisions were made. In June of 1787 the convention of the Ministerium resolved "that the so-called Gospels and Epistles (except for those for Minor Festivals), be printed and bound with the new Hymn Book."[38] With the dissolution of the partnership between Peter Liebert and Michael Billmeyer, the firm which had printed the hymnbook, the rights of publication were given to Billmeyer who continued to publish it. Additional printings of the *Erbauliche Liedersammlung* include those of 1786, 1795, 1803, 1811, 1812, 1814, 1818, and 1829.

The *Choralbuch*
for the *Erbauliche Liedersammlung*

The necessity for a volume to provide music for the organist for use with Muhlenberg's hymnal of 1786, since the *Erbauliche Liedersammlung* contained only words, was soon evident.[39] By 1794 the convention of the Ministerium took steps to correct this matter with the following resolution.

> Resolved, that Dr. Helmuth, F. A. Muhlenberg, Esq., and Mr. Moller, of Philadelphia, be a committee to publish in German papers a plan for the publication of a tune-book, in order that other preachers who have experience in such work may express their opinions as to how such a useful book is to be best arranged; and that then the said committee proceed with the publication.[40]

No further mention is made of the committee or its activity until some 17 years later. By this time both F. A. Muhlenberg—second son of Heinrich Melchior Muhlenberg noted for his political activities—and John Christopher Moller (1765-1803)—German-born composer, organist, recit-alist, and publisher who served as organist of St. Michael-Zion Lutheran Church in Philadelphia from 1790 to 1794—had died. Apparently there was a possibility that the chorale book was to be printed by the congregation in Philadelphia rather than by the Ministerium itself, for in 1811

> Dr. Helmuth reported concerning a [new] "Choralbuch," which was to be printed in Philadelphia, and to contain 220 tunes for our Hymn Book, and wished that it might be introduced generally into all our congregations. The Synod, for its part, promised heartily to support it, in case the corporation of the Ev. Luth. congregation in Philadelphia retained the copyright.[41]

The chorale book finally appeared in 1813, published by the Philadelphia congregation, as the *Choral-Buch fuer die*

Erbauliche Liedersammlung der Deutschen Evan-gelisch-Lutherischen Gemeinden in Nord-Amerika.[42] The scope of the original plan had been somewhat enlarged, for the *Choral-Buch* contained 265 musical settings consisting of melody with figured bass, a practice in line with similar volumes printed in Germany at that time, such as the "Freylinghausen" or "Halle" hymnal. The isometric form of the chorale melodies was predominant. This was the first official Lutheran chorale book to be printed in America.

The texts of Muhlenberg's hymnal of 1786 reflected the pietistically oriented confessionalism with which Muhlenberg had been imbued in Germany and which he sought to preserve in the New World. The *Choral-Buch* of 1813 paralleled the hymnbook with its transplanting of the isometric versions of the chorales to America. In this manner the hymnody of German Pietism, both textually and musically, was carried to America and, in significant ways, helped to shape later developments in American Lutheran hymnody and hymnals.

4

Early Attempts at English and German Lutheran Hymnals

The development of German-language hymnals and hymnody for the American Lutheran churches was only one part of the picture. From the very first, beginning with Muhlenberg himself, there were those who saw the necessity of providing a hymnody in English, the language of the new home for the countless German immigrants who were streaming to the New World. The matter of providing American Lutherans with a suitable English language hymnody brought into focus a unique challenge as well as a unique temptation.

On one hand, if the church's hymnody was to be distinctly Lutheran, it would have to find a way of relating itself to its historic and confessional heritage of the 16th century. This meant, in part, suitable translations of that body of 16th-century hymnody which developed from the impulse of the Reformation, the Lutheran chorale. On the other hand, the church's hymnody needed to avoid the indiscriminate absorbing of the sectarian hymnody of the surrounding denominations in America, which was largely Calvinistic in origin and which often reflected theological understandings at variance with Lutheranism. A too-amiable ecumenism could only do great violence to the integrity of the church's hymnody. Both of these situations presented problems and challenges for the development of a suitable English-language hymnody for American Lutherans.

Both of these problems—that of translations and that of the absorption of sectarian hymnody—were more radically acute for the developing tradition of English language hymnody for Lutherans in America. For German hymnody, the problem of translation was non-existent. In addition, the matter of an indiscriminate absorption of alien or contradictory elements from surrounding denominations was largely diminished by the cultural isolation that the German language provided. The difficulties that these factors raised for an English language hymnody were more crucial. Rationalism—which became increasingly influential in the late 18th and early 19th centuries—failed to see any theological necessity for relating to the historic heritage of Lutheran hymnody, suggesting that much of it was theologically irrelevant. It suggested, moreover, that the task of providing faithful translations was a virtually impossible linguistic task. Unionism, on the other hand, was largely content to absorb whatever English hymnody was at hand, hymnody which was largely Calvinistic in character and origin.

The difficulties which these factors raised for the development of an English-language hymnody for American Lutherans decisively determined the shape of that hymnody for the better part of the 19th century. The course of the struggle for a confessional Lutheran hymnody was largely determined by the church's attitude at any particular time over against these two factors.

Muhlenberg and the *Psalmodia Germanica*

It was readily apparent that the exclusive use of the German language limited the opportunities for outreach open to the Lutheran congregations of 18th century America. While many German-speaking immigrants felt that the preservation of the German language, particularly in public worship, was a necessary ingredient in the conservation and preservation of their faith, others among them felt differently. Throughout the latter decades of the 18th century and the early decades of the 19th century many Lutherans were torn between those who would "boldly adopt English in order to win America, and those who, on the other hand, feared to embrace English lest they be lost in America."[1]

This was a problem which from the beginning affected the ministry of Heinrich Melchior Muhlenberg. In the course of his ministry, Muhlenberg employed, at various times, three languages—German, English, and Dutch—and the hymnody that was familiar to a group at home in one language was not always familiar to a group at home in another. To facilitate congregational singing in English, Muhlenberg often had to read the words of the hymn and sing them for the congregation.

> Having only one copy of the English hymn book containing our hymns, I had to read each stanza separately and sing it for them. I soon discovered that the English people did not know our tunes, so I selected familiar English melodies which fitted some of our Lutheran hymns.[2]

Describing the situation in Hackinsack where he had gone to preach on July 21, 1751, Muhlenberg gives the following account.

> They are not able to sing even the best-known hymns and the miserable lamentable noise they make sounds more like a confused quarrel than a melody. . . . I preached in English on the Prodigal Son, Luke 15, and we sang Jesu, deine tiefe Wunden, from our [Lutheran] English hymnbook. The hymn and melody were unknown, so I read each verse aloud and sang it for them. Several women with a soft, melodious voice joined in and made a pleasing harmony which quite enraptured the people.[3]

The English Lutheran hymnbook to which Muhlenberg refers—and which was undoubtedly the first English collection of Lutheran hymns used in America—was the *Psalmodia Germanica*,[4] a German psalmody translated from the high German and printed in two parts in London in 1722 and 1725. A second edition, combining the two parts, was printed in 1732. The translations were apparently the work of John Christian Jacobi (1670–1750), Organist and Keeper of the Royal German St. James Chapel in London.[5] This chapel, together with St. Mary's of Savoy, became "the spiritual home of thousands of . . . German Lutheran emigrants while they tarried in London"[6] on their way to Pennsylvania. While there is no evidence that the *Psalmodia Germanica* was originally designed for a particular church or congregation, it is apparent that, soon after its publication, it was used in just this manner. The Preface to the third edition published in London in 1756 speaks of the success of the collection and its acceptance "here in London and in the British Settlements in the West Indies."[7]

The *Psalmodia Germanica* was an attempt to translate into English a portion of the great body of German hymnody from the Reformation. Jacobi himself had translated eleven hymns by Luther and eight by Paul Gerhardt which appeared in the first edition. Its immediate purpose was undoubtedly to be of help to the Lutherans in London, as well as to serve the stream of immigrants passing through, most of them on their way to the New World. John Haberkorn, publisher of the 1765 edition, points to the difficulties of the task of translation—and to his conviction that Jacobi had been equal to the task—in his Preface to this collection.

> To translate Spiritual Hymns out of one language into another, in preserving the metres and by course the tunes as well as the spirit of the original, must be allowed to be a very different task; but to execute this task in a number of them sufficient for the different purposes of public and private devotion, seems to me a merit equal, if not superior to that of many original workers, and an unexceptionable proof of an uncommon perseverance and piety in the author.[8]

A sample of Jacobi's work from the *Psalmodia Germanica* is

his translation of the first stanza of Luther's "A mighty fortress."

> God is our Refuge in Distress,
> Our strong Defense and Armour,
> He's present, when we're comfortless,
> In Storms he is our Harbour;
> Th'infernal Enemy
> Look! how enrag'd is he!
> He now exerts his Force
> To stop the GospelCourse;
> Who can withstyand this Tyrant?[29]

The third edition contained 127 hymns of which 33 were contained in a Supplement added to this edition. The tunes to which these hymns were to be sung represent a catalog of many of the finest Reformation melodies.[10] Commenting particularly on the melodies of this collection almost a century later, William Morton Reynolds could remark:

> Here we have such well known melodies as the following: "Wie soll ich dich empfangen;" "Helft mir Gottes Guete preisen;" "Mein Vater zeuge mich, dein Kind;" "Christus der uns selig macht;" "Jesu deine heil'ge Wunden;" "O Lamm Gottes unschuldig;" "Da Jesus an dem Kreuze stand;" "O Traurigkeit;" "Christ lag in Todesbanden;" "Zeuch ein zu deinen Thoren;" "Allein Gott in der Hoeh' sei Ehr;" "Gott der Vater wohn uns bei;" "Nun danket alle Gott;" and more than a hundred others, which embrace the great body of the sublime church tunes of Germany. To have done this is no small achievement, and entitles the Psalmodia Germanica to our lasting gratitude.[11]

From the viewpoint of the development of a Lutheran hymnody in the English language this hymnbook is important for two reasons: 1) its use by Muhlenberg as he reached out to serve an increasingly English-speaking constituency, and 2) its role in the development of the first English language Lutheran hymnbook that was to be printed in America. The archaic character and seeming lack of grace of the texts, reminiscent of the texts of the Bay Psalm Book of 1640, made the *Psalmodia Germanica* an easy target for criticism by later generations—both Lutheran and others—who had grown accustomed to a more elegant literary style and expression.

> These translations would undoubtedly be very acceptable to the pious worshippers whose knowledge of the English language did not at once revolt against its numerous Germanisms and other offenses against idiomatic English as well as poetical taste and the higher graces of composition.[12]

Even Louis Benson, while admitting that the *Psalmodia Germanica* "included many of the best Lutheran hymns," noted that "had the English versions been of better quality, [the *Psalmodia Germanica*] might have afforded a nucleus for the development here of a characteristic Lutheran hymnody."[13] Luther Reed characterized the literary style of this collection as "so deficient, indeed often so ludicrous"[14] that he could not bring himself to include anything of Jacobi's work in the *Service Book and Hymnal* of 1958. Regardless of any lack of grace in the translations from German to English, the subsequent history of English Lutheran hymnody in America strongly suggests that the rationalism of early 19th century Lutheranism together with a developing concern for "literary excellence"—a theme to which we shall return—were to play significant roles in the development of Lutheran hymnody in America. For those Lutheran churches that sought to adapt to the English language in the New World, both rationalism and the developing concern for "literary excellence" would lead them to turn them away from the rich heritage of the confessional hymnody of the German Lutheran Reformation.

Kunze's *A Hymn and Prayer Book*:
The First English Lutheran Hymnal Published in America

While Pennsylvania remained the stronghold of German-speaking Lutheranism,[15] it was the state of New York that produced the first English hymnbook for Lutherans in America. The man responsible for this hymnbook was John Christopher Kunze. Kunze (1744–1807) was born in Saxony and educated at Halle (under G. A. Francke) and the University of Leipzig. He began his pastoral work in Philadelphia in 1770 as an associate of H. M. Muhlenberg at St. Michael and Zion congregations. In 1771 he married Muhlenberg's second daughter, Margaretta Henrietta, succeeding Muhlenberg as chief pastor in 1779. In 1773 Kunze started a *Seminarium* in Philadelphia for the training of native pastors, which closed in 1776 because of the Revolutionary War. In 1784 Kunze accepted a call to New York where in the same year he united the old Dutch church (Trinity) and the German Lutheran Church (Christ) into the United German Lutheran Churches in the city of New York. He organized the New York Ministerium in 1786 and became its first president, continuing in office until his death in 1807. He was one of the most eminent scholars of his day, a specialist in oriental languages, and in 1779—together with Thomas Jefferson, Anthony Wayne, and George Washington—Kunze was elected a member of the American Philosophical Society.

Kunze was deeply concerned with the development of an English-speaking Lutheranism already while in Philadelphia. His ardent advocacy for the use of English in worship undoubtedly contributed to the alienation of another colleague there, J. C. Helmuth. Helmuth (1745–1825) was a product of Halle who came to America and eventually became an associate pastor of St. Michael and Zion congregations in Philadelphia where Kunze was the pastor. In 1786 he was elected president of the Pennsylvania Ministerium and, after Kunze resigned at Zion and St. Michael's congregation, Helmuth became the chief pastor. All this was undoubtedly involved in Kunze's decision to accept the call to New York in 1784.

In New York Kunze set about to reinstate English services begun as early as 1751 by Muhlenberg and continued by his successor Weyland, but apparently dropped some time before Kunze appeared on the scene. Kunze himself tried to preach in English, but he soon gave it up because he found it too difficult. It was about a decade later when an available candidate who could preach in English appeared on the scene—George Strebeck.

In 1795 Kunze published *A Hymn and Prayer-Book*: for the use of such Lutheran Churches as use the English Language.[16] The hymns for this hymnbook were compiled, with a few exceptions, from two hymnals that Kunze had at his disposal: the *Psalmodia Germanica* and a Moravian collection of hymns published in London in 1789.[17] Writing in the Preface to this collection, Kunze states,

> Most all of the hymns are translations from the German, and were used before in their churches. All except those in the appendix are taken from printed books, particularly the German Psalmody, printed in London and reprinted at New-York, by H. Gaine, 1756, with which many serious English persons have been greatly delighted; and from an excellent collection of the Moravian Brethren, printed in London, 1789. In the appendix only have I taken the liberty to add a few of my own, and of the Rev. Messrs. Ernst's and Strebeck's, both translations and original compositions.[18]

Of the 240 hymns in this collection, including 20 in the appendix), approximately 150 were translations from the German, about 75 from the *Psalmodia Germanica* and the same number from the Moravian collection. Of the hymns from English sources, texts of Watts, Wesley, and Newton were the most prominent. However, many of the hymns from the Moravian collection were from Lutheran sources, particularly from Paul Gerhardt. Thus the compilation of this first English Lutheran hymnal to be made in America was accomplished in such a manner so that, as Frederick Bird has pointed out, " . . . [what has occurred in no subsequent hymnal,] more than half the contents are of Lutheran origin."[19]

The appendix to Kunze's collection contained six hymns of Kunze's own composition, five by George Strebeck, his assistant at the New York congregation, and four by John Frederick Ernst, pastor of the Athens, New York congregation in the Albany region. The attempt at writing new hymns in English apparently proved too much for Kunze and his associates, as the following example from Kunze's own hand illustrates.

> Holy King Zion's, look down, thee me offer
> Honor with love in harmonious strains;
> Purchased so dearly we never will suffer,
> Blood of ungratefulness running in veins,
> Lo! loving master, thy pupils attend them!
> Cherish thy chosen few, Lord, and attend them.[20]

Nevertheless, Kunze was the first editor of an English Lutheran hymnbook in America and, together with his associates, the first writers of English hymns by Lutherans in America.

In spite of its awkward and inelegant translations, Nicum could speak highly of Kunze's hymnbook as possessing a "strong Lutheran character."[21] Even allowing for the problems he encountered with the language, the hymnal Kunze produced was a remarkable example of a Lutheran hymnbook that, from many points of view, was unequalled for almost three-quarters of a century. Bird's evaluation, written 70 years later in 1865 placed Kunze's collection in the context of its time:

> If we allow for the remote time and the peculiar circumstances, remembering that the book was gotten up by one or two isolated German clergymen just beginning to use English, and necessarily unacquainted, to any considerable extent, either with the language or its Hymnology, we shall

see that good Dr. Kunze did his work better, in proportion to his abilities and opportunities, than most who have followed him.[22]

The Efforts of Strebeck and Williston

While Kunze's congregation—Christ Church in New York—remained essentially a German-speaking one, Zion Church in New York, formed in 1786 out of Kunze's German congregation with George Strebeck as its pastor, became the first English-speaking Lutheran congregation in America.[23] Strebeck was apparently unhappy with Kunze's earlier efforts in his English collection of hymns, and alleging the "unsuitableness of the metres of our English Lutheran Hymn Book, published in 1795," and at the request of his own congregation,[24] Strebeck prepared *A Collection of evangelical Hymns, made from different authors and collections, for the English Lutheran Church, in New York,* which appeared in 1797[25] containing 304 hymns.

From the perspective of historic Lutheranism, Strebeck's effort was a dramatic departure even from the standard set by Kunze just two years earlier. Of the 304 hymns in Strebeck's collection, only 48 hymns were retained from Kunze's collection, and of these only 10 were translations of German hymns. Of the remaining hymns about one-half were taken from Isaac Watts, about one-fifth from Charles Wesley, and about one-eighth from the "Olney Hymns" of Newton and Cowper.[26] Even Strebeck seemed somewhat apologetic for the un-Lutheran character of the collection for he remarks that he hopes that "none will be so bigoted to mere name, as to censure us for making selections from authors of this description."[27] Within a few years Strebeck had carried the bulk of his congregation over to the Protestant Episcopal Church.

Strebeck's successor at Zion was Ralph Williston, who became pastor in 1805. He was requested by his congregation to compile a new hymnbook, since Strebeck's earlier collection was no longer available, and its "obvious deficiency"[28] apparently did not warrant a reprinting. A few years earlier, in 1803, the New York Ministerium had named pastors Kunze, F. H. Quitman, and George Strebeck as a committee to prepare an official English hymnbook for its congregations.[29] The subsequent minutes of the New York Ministerium, however, contain no report of the committee in the years immediately following, and with the desertion of Strebeck to the Episcopal Church and the death of Kunze in 1807, apparently nothing was done.

In the ensuing vacuum, Williston produced *A choice Selection of evangelical Hymns, from various authors: for the use of the English Evangelical-Lutheran Church in New York*.[30] It appeared in 1806 and consisted largely—as did Strebeck's collection—of hymns of Watts, Charles Wesley, and other Evangelical writers. Kunze wrote a brief Preface to the collection, but in spite of his assurance that in the selection of hymns "none is found among them dissonant to our doctrine, or incompatible with the spirit of genuine godliness," according to Benson. "Neither its arrangements nor contents suggests Lutheranism. It was in fact a good evangelical collection and was widely used within the New York Ministerium."[31]

With Strebeck's defection to the Episcopal Church and with no activity on the part of the other members of the committee appointed to implement the New York Ministerium's resolution of 1803 to provide a new hymnbook, it may be that Williston felt that his collection would fill this need. However, in spite of Kunze's endorsement, there is no indication that this was an official collection endorsed by the New York Ministerium. Williston, at one time a Methodist, soon followed Strebeck into the Episcopal Church, taking his congregation with him and reincorporating the only English Lutheran Church in New York as Zion Protestant Episcopal Church in 1810.

Kunze's *A Hymn and Prayer-Book* of 1795 was, in spite of a later generation's criticism of its literary style, a Lutheran hymnbook in the truest sense of the word. The hymnbooks of Strebeck in 1797 and Williston in 1806, however, gave the first indications of the path that English Lutheran hymnals were to follow in the years ahead. That path was to give more and more exclusive attention to the work of English hymn writers—Watts, Wesley, and other Evangelical writers who followed them—at the expense of Lutheranism's own historic heritage, and thus to make English Lutheran hymnals less and less Lutheran in character. In choosing this path, a choice encouraged by and in turn encouraging the tendency in New York toward union with the Episcopal Church, English Lutheran hymnody took the first step toward the anglicizing of its hymnody that was to reach its maturity by the middle of the 19th century and from which it has not yet completely recovered.

By the time the New York Ministerium produced its own English hymnal, J. C. Kunze had passed from the scene and with him any concern for a confessionally oriented hymnody. By 1807 the presidency of the New York Ministerium had passed to Dr. F. H. Quitman, a leading exponent of the rationalistic tendencies of his day. With the work of Quitman, Lutheran hymnody in America was to fall to its lowest level.

Paul Henkel's Two Hymnals

Two additional hymnals, one German and one English, which appeared early in Lutheranism's history in America, were the work of the great home missionary of the early years of the 19th century, Paul Henkel (1754–1825). Henkel came from a long line of pastors, his great-grandfather, Anthony Jacob Henkel, being regarded as the "founder of the old Lutheran churches in Philadelphia and Germantown."[32] Paul Henkel took part in the organization of the North Carolina Synod in 1803, of the Ohio Synod in 1818, and the Tennessee Synod in 1820.

While a pastor in New Market, Virginia, he prepared *Das Neu eingerichtete Gesangbuch*, a collection of 246 hymns published in 1810. [33] A second edition was issued in 1812 that included three additional hymns. The book, which provided at least one hymn for each Sunday of the church year in addition to a number of festivals, was an undistinguished collection of hymns, many of them apparently written by Henkel himself. It was most likely used only by a small number of congregations.

A few years later, in 1816, Henkel published a collection of hymns in English entitled *Church Hymn Book*[34] containing 347 hymns, followed by a complete metrical Psalter from Watts and others. The first part is a "Hymnal Companion to the Liturgy" with "Hymns adapted to the Gospel and Epistle throughout the ecclesiastical year."[35] Typical of Henkel's texts was the following hymn designated as a "Hymn for the Gospel" for Quasimodogeniti Sunday, the First Sunday after Easter, based on John 20:19-31.

> When the disciples refuge sought
> To shun the stubborn Jews;
> When they had neither hope nor thought
> They hear'd a welcome new's.
>
> Their doors were bolted, bar'd & lock'd,
> To guard them in their fears;
> The Savior neither call'd nor knock'd,
> But suddenly appears.
>
> My peace be unto you he said,
> My peace to you is giv'n;
> You need not doubt nor be affraid,
> I am your Lord from heav'n.
>
> That they might be convinc'd and know;
> And fully satisfied;
> His wounded hands to them did show;
> Likewise his pierced side.
>
> Thus with all saints it is the case,
> When Jesus is withdrawn;

When he appears to hide his face,
Then all our joys are gone.

Like the disciples they feel sad,
Like them they feel distress'd;
A view of Jesus makes them glad,
And sooth's their minds to rest,

Let us assemble, watch and pray,
As faithful servants do!
Till Jesus visits us and say,
My peace be unto you.

The inclusion of a complete metrical psalter in this collection is evidence of the general impact of metrical psalmody in early America. Of particular interest is the inclusion by Henkel, at the end of the psalter, of "Pope's Universal Prayer," which began:

Father of All! in ev'ry age,
In ev'ry clime ador'd,
By saint, by savage, and by sage,
Jehovah, Jove, or Lord!

Thou great First Cause, least understood;
Who all my sense confin'd.
To know but this, that Thou art God,
And that myself am blind:

Yet gave me, in this dark estate,
To see the good from ill;
And binding nature fast to fate.
Left free the human will.

Benson's characterization of this collection as "nothing more than didactic prose broken up into short phrases that serve as lines of verse"[36] is essentially correct. A large portion of the contents were apparently written by Paul Henkel himself.[37]

Henkel's *Church Book* reached a total of four editions, the last of which was published in 1857.[38] This hymnbook had little, if any, effect on the general development of Lutheran hymnody in America, its use being confined largely to the Tennessee Synod, formed in 1820, and the congregations which it served.

5

Movements Toward Accommodation: Rationalism, Unionism, and Revivalism

Three forces that most profoundly affected the development of American Lutheran hymnody in the first half of the 19th century were rationalism, unionism, and revivalism. The spread of these movements, in America as in Germany, was accompanied by a general toning down of Lutheran convictions and by a relaxing of sound Lutheran principles. [1] The revised constitution of the Pennsylvania Ministerium adopted in 1792, for example, excised all references to the Lutheran Confessions, and in the New York Ministerium the presidency passed into the hands of Dr. Frederick H. Quitman, an avowed disciple of Johann Salomo Semler, the "father of rationalism" at Halle.

Rationalism, which sought in human reason the answer to many religious questions, was, in part, a reaction to the excesses of German Pietism of the late 17th and early 18th centuries, which sought religious certainty in human feelings and the emotions. German rationalism is closely associated with the name of Johann Salomo Semler (1725–91) who, through his pupils, had a direct impact on American Lutheranism in the first half of the 19th century. Raised a Pietist, Semler came under the influence of a developing rationalism as a student at the University of Halle, ultimately returning to Halle as a professor of theology where he taught from 1752–79. Among the many effects of this movement, rationalism brought into question the historical and doctrinal authority of the church, sought to bring Christian belief in line with human reason, and fostered an indifference and often outright hostility toward the liturgical practices and historic hymnody of the church.

The movement toward the union of various churches that developed at this time was due, in part, to the spirit of religious indifference fostered by the inroads of rationalism, in part because union with other church bodies was often the line of least resistance, especially among groups of immigrants that shared a common ethnic heritage, but also because it frequently appeared to be the most prudent course in the common cause of evangelizing America. In New York the trend was toward union between Lutherans and Episcopalians, while in Pennsylvania the tendency was toward union between the Lutheran and the Reformed churches.

Rationalism and Quitman's *Collection* of 1814

Rationalism was to have a substantive effect among Lutherans in America. While it was resisted by some, it became a significant influence in the Lutheran Church in the years before and after the turn of the century. In 1792, for example, the Pennsylvania Ministerium deleted all references to the Lutheran Confessions from its constitution. There was also no reference to the Confessions in the ordination rites for Lutheran pastors in this period; in the Pennsylvania Ministerium's Order for Baptism there was no reference to the Trinity; and in its Order of Holy Communion various liberties were taken with the Words of Institution.[2] Doctrinal laxity and indifference were widespread.

Perhaps the most important and influential American Lutheran who aggressively espoused the cause of rationalism was Frederick Henry Quitman (1760–1832). Born in Iserloh, Germany, he studied at Halle under Johann Semler. Ordained in 1783 at the Lutheran Consistory in Amsterdam,

Holland, he served the Dutch Lutheran colony in Curacao in the West Indies. He came to the United States in 1795, serving several pastorates for more than 30 years, and served as second president of the New York Ministerium, succeeding Kunze, from 1807–25. He was well-educated, persuasive, and a thoroughgoing rationalist, denying the authority of the Bible and the Lutheran Confessions.

As early as 1803, the New York Ministerium had appointed a committee consisting of Dr. Kunze, Frederick Quitman, and Georg Strebeck for the production of an English hymnbook. The death of Kunze and the secession of Strebeck to the Episcopal Church resulted in no action being taken. By 1811 Quitman had been president of the New York Ministerium for four years, and in that year the Ministerium resolved to produce a new English hymnbook.[3] In 1812 the Ministerium, convening at Rhinebeck, appointed a committee for the hymnbook,[4] and two years later it appeared as *A Collection of Hymns, and a Liturgy, for the use of the Evangelical Lutheran Churches*.[5] The hymnbook contained 520 hymns and was primarily the work of F. H. Quitman, president of the New York Ministerium, together with his associates, Drs. Wackerhagen[6] and Mayer. Nicum succinctly characterized Quitman's hymnbook as follows: "The new hymnbook was a vague and completely un-Lutheran work."[7]

Quitman's book was marked by two important features. First, it rejected almost completely the heritage of the Lutheran chorale, apparently finding the chorale's vigorous evangelical confessionalism unsuited to the theological currents of the day, and turned almost exclusively to English sources. Second, those hymns that were included were freely altered to conform with the rationalistic tendency of the time.

Although Quitman, Wackerhagen, and Mayer had all been intimately associated with Kunze, this hymnbook "almost entirely rejected the German element, and drew its hymns from sources well-nigh exclusively English."[8] Whether the possibility of translating the Lutheran chorales into English was regarded as a hopeless venture, or whether their vigorous confessionalism was too much for the rationalistic ideas of the time, is difficult to determine. Undoubtedly both factors were involved. An additional factor was the attraction of union with the Episcopal Church, a factor that contributed little toward furthering the Lutheran heritage of the chorale.

Quitman readily acknowledged the contribution of German hymnody to the German Lutheran congregations in America.

> The Lutheran church in Germany is distinguished for its attachment to sacred music, and is possessed of, perhaps, the best and most numerous collections of hymns extant in the Christian world. From this source, our German congregations in the United States have derived abundant supplies.[9]

But regarding the previous compilations of English hymns for Lutherans in America, Quitman held a lower opinion.

> The prevalence of the English language, however, makes it necessary for many members of our communion to conduct their public worship, altogether, or in part, in that language, and of course to provide for them a compilation of English hymns. This has indeed been already attempted by several individuals. But as the selection published by them, evidently admit of great improvement, another was ordered to be prepared by a committee appointed for that purpose by the Lutheran Synod of the State of New York, convened at Rhinebeck in September, A. D. 1812.[10]

The "great improvement" that Quitman felt was necessary to improve the hymnody of his day was twofold. On the one hand it was necessary to bring it into line with the theology of the time, a theology largely characterized by "its high Arminian view of human potentiality, its ethical moralisms, its sweetly reasonable descriptions of a benevolent deity, its criticism of dogma, especially the Trinity."[11] Even while admitting its literary and intellectual qualities, Luther Reed acknowledged that regarding Quitman's collection, "its emphasis upon the ethical rather than the devotional was in agreement with the point of view and the practice of New England Unitarianism." [12] On the other hand Quitman was concerned with the poor literary quality of the work of his predecessors, especially Kunze. The relative infelicity of Kunze's translations did little to reflect favorably on the entire attempt to translate the historic Lutheran heritage into English. Quitman's own sensitivity to the English language, clearly evident in his Preface, could only have been repulsed by these earlier and cruder attempts.

To accomplish the task of accommodating his hymnal to the theology of the day, Quitman and his co-workers showed "no hesitation in altering hymns that did not coincide with their ideas."[13] Quitman's treatment of Isaac Watts' "Alas! and did my Savior bleed" illustrates his editorial procedure. The second stanza

> Was it for crimes that I had done,
> He groaned upon the tree?
> Amazing pity, grace unknown,
> And love beyond degree!

was summarily omitted. Of this omission Reynolds says, "The doctrine of the Atonement so strongly and beautifully expressed in the verse just quoted was one of the most offensive to the Socinianism of the times, and we are not, therefore, surprised to find it suppressed by this summary process."[14] Regarding the divinity of Christ, Quitman is careful to alter Watts' text in stanza three from "When God the Almighty Maker died" (as found in Kunze's hymnbook) to "When Christ, the mighty Savior died." Commenting on the titles of the various sections of the hymnbook, Reynolds says:

We have "The Mission and Nativity of Christ," "The Office and Mediation of Christ," "The Sufferings and death of Christ," "The Kingdom and Church of Christ," all implying the supreme divinity of Christ, but find very few hymns which a Unitarian like Dr. Channing, or a high Arian might not sing with as much satisfaction as an orthodox believer in the doctrine of the Trinity. Of course, we nowhere find a clear recognition of the doctrine of the Trinity.[15]

"There is no hymn distinctly devoted to the divinity of Christ, not even a doxology."[16] The same author further suggests that "we fail to recognize a distinct statement of the doctrine of Original Sin or Innate Depravity."[17] Regarding hymns for Baptism and the Lord's Supper, it is Reynold's view that "there is nothing that would distinguish this [hymnbook] from a Presbyterian or a Methodist collection of hymns, and Watts has here much more of the Lutheran spirit than these hymns breathe."[18]

Quitman's *A Collection of Hymns, and a Liturgy* also dispensed with the church year as the organizing principle of the hymnbook. Where Muhlenberg's *Erbauliche Lieder-sammlung* gave pride of place to the church year, Quitman substituted an arrangement according to various topics reflecting the type of organization to be found in any number of Reformed hymnals of the day. The "Order and Subjects of the Hymns" in Quitman's hymnbook was as follows.

Praise and Thanksgiving
Character and Perfections of God
Works of God in Nature
Divine Providence and Government
Mission and Nativity of Christ
Office and Mediation of Christ
Example of Christ
Sufferings and Death of Christ
Resurrection and Glory of Christ
Kingdom and Church of Christ
The Influence of God's holy Spirit
The Scriptures
Supplication for the divine favour and assistance
The Danger and Misery of Sin
Repentance and Conversion
The Joy and Happiness of true Christians
The Christian Character and Life, in general
Faith

Duties of Piety
Personal Duties
Social Duties
Public Worship
Baptism
The Lord's Supper
Particular Occasions and Circumstances
The Troubles of Life
Death
Resurrection
Judgment and End of the World
Heaven

By 1834 a new edition of Quitman's collection was prepared by a committee of which Dr. P. F. Mayer, pastor of St. John's Lutheran Church in Philadelphia, was the chairman.[19] Apparently the work was largely that of Mayer and appeared as *Additional Hymns* in 1834. It added 179 hymns, but there was no material change in the tone or spirit of the revised work.

> The whole is distinguished by that refined and correct taste . . . more unction and a higher tone of literary composition . . . but we find . . . no special addition to the orthodoxy of the book.[20]

That this revised edition was indeed no advance on the first edition is painfully evident from the following stanza that appeared as hymn number 349:

> Who with another's eye can read?
> Or worship by another's creed?
> Trusting thy grace, we form our own,
> And bow to thy commands alone.[21]

Quitman's hymnbook also reflects the aversion to any prescribed liturgy on the part of those who were leaving the Lutheran tradition behind. While including "forms of prayer, with necessary directions and addresses to congregations," Quitman clearly states that the use of these forms is left entirely to the discretion of congregations and ministers, the Synod having no design to make them binding upon any in connection with us, but judging that the leaders of the devotions of their brethren should be at perfect liberty to address the throne of grace in their own words.[22]

The withdrawal of the Pennsylvania Ministerium from any active concern for the development of an English Lutheran hymnody more consonant with Lutheranism's historic heritage left the field largely to the New York Ministerium and to Quitman's "Collection" of 1814. While extensively used, Quitman's hymnal never became the "common hymnbook" of Muhlenberg's vision. Fourteen years after the appearance of Quitman's hymnal the General Synod attempted to provide a hymnal more truly "common" and more truly Lutheran.

Mention must be made of two choralbooks that appeared about the time of Quitman's hymnbook and which, while neither was in any way an official collection authorized by the New York Synod, had a passing connection with Quitman's collection. The first is *Chorale Book*[23] of 1816 by John Jacob Eckhard (1757–1833). While this collection was based, in part, on an earlier manuscript collection of 1809 and was primarily designed for Episcopal use, particularly at St. Michael's in Charleston, South Carolina, Eckhard apparently hoped it might be used as well in Lutheran congregations, for it included "an Index of the particular metres suited to the Evangelical Lutheran Hymn Book."[24] This Index contained only 66 hymns from the New York collection, and thus was hardly in a position to make a significant contribution toward providing settings for the 520 hymns in Quitman's *A Collection of Hymns, and a Liturgy* of 1814.

A collection that came much closer to supplying the need for a chorale book for Quitman's hymn book was *A Collection of Church Tunes* by Peter Erben (1771–1861). While there is no date on the title page, nor is there a copyright date, this collection was apparently published in 1817, possibly 1818. The collection contained 109 selections and included examples drawn from Erben's earlier Episcopal and Reformed tune book collections, from the repertory of early American psalmody, a smaller number from the repertory of German chorales, together with a few tunes apparently written by Erben himself.[25]

While neither of these two chorale books were prepared under the direction of the New York Synod nor authorized for use by that body, they were undoubtedly used to some extent by some Lutheran congregations. The parallel between the name of the New York hymnbook and Peter Erben's choralbook (*A Collection of Hymns, and a liturgy* and *A Collection of Church Tunes*) is probably more than just a coincidence. Both Eckhard's and Erben's collections were published in the years immediately following the publication of Quitman's hymnal and both were probably to some extent designed to capitalize on the market provided by those congregations who would use Quitman's collection.

Both collections followed in the immediate wake of the publication of the first German Lutheran choralebook published in America, the *Choral-buch fuer die Erbauliche Liedersammlung* of 1813. It would be almost 60 years until the first English Lutheran hymnbook with music would be authorized by the General Council in 1872.

Unionism and *Das Gemeinschaftliche Gesangbuch* of 1817

The attraction of Lutheran and Reformed churches in America to each other in the early years of the 19th century can be readily understood. Rationalism had tended to obliterate confessional differences, or at least made them seem unimportant. From the early 17th century, the official state policy in Prussia, homeland of many of the German-Americans, was one of union between Lutheran and Reformed churches.[26] Moreover as both Lutherans and Reformed congregations began to make plans for the celebration of the 300th anniversary of the Reformation in 1817, it was inevitable that there would be conversations concerning any number of joint activities. As Lutheran and Reformed congregations often shared the same church building for the conducting of services and "common hymn books" provided an answer to a practical problem, the request for hymnals that could be used jointly by Lutheran and Reformed congregations alike could not be far behind.

The subject of a common hymnal for Lutheran and Reformed became a matter of public concern at a meeting of the Pennsylvania Ministerium already in 1814.

> It was announced to the Synod that at a meeting of preachers of different denominations (held the previous Fall at Hummelstown, Dauphin County), the desire was expressed that there might be put through the press a common little hymn book, for use in public service, containing about 250 hymns, which shall be chosen from both of the new hymn books. It is desired to know whether the Evangelical Lutheran Synod, in connection with the Reformed Synod, is willing to undertake the matter, or in case this cannot be done, whether the said meeting has permission to do it on its own responsibility.[27]

The matter was postponed until the following year when the Ministerium in 1815, meeting at Fredericktown, took the following stand regarding so-called "common" hymnbooks.

> Concerning the common [gemeinschaftliche] little hymnbook, for use in the public service of the German Protestant congregations, it was resolved, that it were best not to have anything to do with the same, and that no member, or several members in our connection have a right to have a new hymn-book prepared or printed, without consent of the Synod.[28]

But the matter was not so easily settled. Lutheran, Reformed and other Protestant congregations in America were making joint plans to celebrate the 300th anniversary of the Reformation. In Germany Frederick Wilhelm III was preparing to proclaim the Prussian Union. The tide of opinion, favoring at least a variety of united activities and at best, hopefully, union, was too great.

In 1817, on the 300th anniversary of the Reformation, there appeared *Das Gemeinschaftliche Gesangbuch, zum gottesdienstlichen Gebrauch der Lutherischen und Reformierten Gemeinden in Nord-America*[29] (The Common Hymn Book for use in the worship of Lutheran and Reformed congregations in North America). It contained 494 hymns, a small collection of prayers, and a listing of the Epistles and Gospels for the Church Year. The purpose of the hymnbook was clearly pointed out in the Preface.

> The salutary purpose of this book is indicated clearly enough on the title page. Where is there a family in our land that, to one degree or another, is not composed of members of both Lutheran and Reformed churches? How welcome a book of this kind must be in every household—a book which not only removes the difficulty that inevitably arises in the public worship of "common churches" from the use of two different books; but also provides an unusual heightening effect in home devotions, when the entire family, just as they read from one Bible, can also praise and laud their God and Savior from one hymnbook. At the same time this book has the purpose of breaking down the wall of partition between Lutherans and Reformed, which is based only on prejudice, and to spread abroad the true spirit of Jesus' religion, the spirit of tolerance and brotherhood, and to unite one Christian with another ever more fervently.[30]

The Preface claimed that in the selection of hymns the "large number of the hymns have been taken from our old hymnals on both sides, especially those which have been commonly recognized and long used as edifying core hymns [Kernlieder]."[31] Luther Reed, offering a contrary evaluation, suggests that the incapacity of the editors was revealed especially "in the omission of the classic hymns of the church and the insertion of weak and frivolous hymns." In fact only one hymn of Luther and 11 by Gerhardt are included, while Gellert, one of the leading hymn writers of the period of rationalism, is represented by 40 hymns.[32]

Another concern was a new arrangement of the contents

of this "common book." From the beginning, Lutheran hymnals had been organized according to the church year, with other hymns following. This collection follows a new plan.

> [W]e now submit that the hymnbooks published in the last 20 years depart from the older books in that they always place in the first section—which contains the dogmatic theology—the teachings concerning the knowledge of God, the creation, the attributes and perfections of God, the Fall, and the sorry consequences thereof, and only then the teaching concerning the consoling salvation through Jesus Christ. We have chosen and retained this arrangement in place of the older one as a more practical one because it is entirely suited to the teaching of the Bible and is also suited to an orderly development of the knowledge of God and Jesus.[33]

This new arrangement, rejecting the church year and substituting an arrangement based on a systematic presentation of religious doctrine, was essentially of Reformed origin. Such an arrangement was perfectly consistent with an approach to worship and congregational song that rejected the Lutheran sacramental heritage of liturgy and worship, that made the sermon increasingly the central act in worship, and that saw the hymnbook as simply a resource to underscore the teaching of a sermon wrenched from any traditional liturgical context. It was an arrangement that was to dominate Lutheran hymnals until the confessional revival would attempt to return Lutheranism and its hymnals to a practice more consistent with its heritage.

As to particular editorial practices, the *Preface* notes that the hymns

> . . . have been retained unchanged when they combined a spiritual content with a purity of expression. Several have been altered where the expression was obscure or was not appropriate, or where it would be prejudicial to edification and devotion. Those which lacked spirituality and grammatical correctness throughout were omitted. In the place of such old hymns which, because of their unknown meter, could never be

sung in most churches, new hymns are given with known melodies whose authors are not only good poets but also practical and pious Christians, for example Lavater, Sturm, Gellert, Cramer, and others.[34]

The first edition carried the endorsement of Augustus Wackerhagen, Dr. C. L. Becker, Daniel Kurz, Frederick D. Schaeffer, and especially Frederick Quitman, who praised its timeliness and urged its introduction into the parishes of his brethren. Typical of the positive response that this collection engendered in those who were attracted to such union efforts was that of Rev. Gottlieb Schober of the North Carolina Synod.

> This meritorious undertaking paves the way to universal harmony, union, and love among our Lutheran and Reformed Churches, removing all the obstacles which hitherto prevented that happy effect, and establishes a uniformity in that part of divine worship which cannot fail to be highly gratifying to all those who consider brotherly love an indispensable attribute of Christianity.[35]

Commenting on Schober's statement some years later, Socrates Henkel placed it in a different perspective.

> No doubt, this insidious course produced, to a considerable extent, for the time being, the effect which the author of those lines so much desired—for the songs and services used in worship exert great influence. But whilst it was doing this, it was aiding in engendering and cultivating a spirit which, as the child of an unjustifiable compromise of principles, ultimately resulted in injuring some of the most vital and fundamental doctrines and elements of the Church, leaving her in that latitudinarian state of indifference and laxness in regard to almost every thing that was regarded as positive and definite, in which she appeared about the beginning of the nineteenth century, without helm or rudder—a deplorable wreck, requiring years for its restoration.[36]

The use of such a "union" hymnbook was furthered some

years later with the publication of the *Neues Gemein-chaftliches Gesangbuch*.[37] Nicum's criticism is direct and to the point.

> This book contained 495 hymns, only eight of which are from the 16th century and of those eight only one of Luther ("Aus tiefer Not"). Two hundred and thirty come from the period of Rationalism. Most importantly, the book is full of the moralistic rhymes of J. Dietrich, who in 1780, together with the rationalist Teller, produced the new Prussian hymn book.[38]

In spite of their obvious weakness, the use of such "common hymnbooks" was widespread, for union churches were common and common hymnbooks were popular.[39] The immediate result of the introduction of these "common books" was the beginning of the displacement of Muhlenberg's *Erbauliche Liedersammlung* by a hymnody that had virtually no relationship to the historic Lutheran hymnody of the 16th century. As a result of the debilitating effects of unionism and rationalism, Lutheran hymnody in America—particularly in Quitman's *A Collection of Hymns, and a Liturgy* and *Das Gemeinschaftliche Gesangbuch*—reached its lowest point. In the broad sweep of American Lutheran hymnody, it was a retrogression from which it would take almost a century to fully recover.

Revivalism and The General Synod's
Hymns, selected and original (1828)

If Quitman's collection of 1814 reflected the inroads of rationalism in American Lutheranism, and the "common hymnbook" of 1817 demonstrated the deleterious effects of unionism on American Lutheran hymnody, it was the hymnals of the General Synod that most clearly showed the impact of the growing attraction of the "new measures" of frontier evangelism. The General Synod of the Evangelical

Lutheran Church in the United States of America, the first federation of Lutheran synods in America, was organized in 1820, its initial membership consisting of the Maryland and Virginia Synod, the New York Ministerium, the North Carolina Synod, and the Pennsylvania Ministerium. The idea of such a general body was first promoted by such men as J. H. C. Helmuth and Gottlieb Schober. It was to be the only such federation among American Lutherans for over 40 years until the formation of the United Synod of the South and the General Council in the 1860s.

The General Synod was an attempt to foster a greater Lutheran self-consciousness; in addition it was a force that, it was hoped, would help prevent the absorption or submergence of Lutheranism in the sectarianism that characterized much of American religious life. Yet from its beginning the General Synod was so broadly "evangelical" that it lost sight of some fundamental elements of Lutheranism. Mention of the Bible and the Lutheran Confessions were intentionally omitted from its constitution; while the Augsburg Confession was regarded as a Lutheran Confession, a distinction was made between fundamental and non-fundamental doctrines, and the Augsburg Confession was to be followed only in fundamental doctrines; and the traditional Lutheran understanding concerning baptism and the Lord's Supper was rejected.

It was in the context of the General Synod that the mid-century conflict developed between "American Lutheranism," advocated by Samuel Simon Schmucker (1799–1873), and a more confessional understanding of Lutheranism.[40] Strongly advocated by S. S. Schmucker, the leading theologian of the General Synod for over 40 years, and others such as Benjamin Kurtz and Samuel Sprecher, "American Lutheranism" was a movement in which Schmucker and others argued for adapting Lutheranism to the American scene to make it more agreeable and palatable in America, in the process abandoning many beliefs and practices more conservative Lutherans held to be at the heart of the faith.

In the 1820s and 1830s, the Second Great Awakening also began to make its influence felt among Lutheran churches as many appropriated the worship style, "new measures," hymns, and songs of the revivalism that was sweeping the country. As Lutheranism spread westward, new synods joined the General Synod, and others, for a variety of reasons dropped out. At the time of the Civil War, a split developed in the General Synod over the issue of slavery, those members of the General Synod favoring slavery seceding to form the United Synod of the South. Ultimately, in 1918, the General Synod became part of the merger of several Lutheran bodies that originated in the planning for the celebration of the 400th anniversary of the Reformation in 1917. The General Synod produced two hymn books, one German and one English. It was the English hymnbook, guided by S. S. Schmucker, leading exponent of "American Lutheranism," that was to be a particularly significant influence on the course of Lutheran hymnody in America at midcentury.

Hymns, Selected and Original of 1828

The organization of the General Synod in 1820 presented a new opportunity for the development of an English Lutheran hymnbook that would avoid the pitfalls that befell some of the earlier attempts at a Lutheran hymnody in the English language. The Pennsylvania Ministerium had no English hymnbook of its own. Quitman's New York collection being used in those congregations of the Pennsylvania Ministerium where English was tolerated.[41] But even within the New York Ministerium the need for something more adequate than Quitman's collection was widely recognized.[42]

Five years after its organization, at a meeting of the General Synod convened at Frederick, Maryland, in 1825, it was resolved to proceed with the preparation of a new English hymnbook.

Resolved, That Dr. Schmucker, Rev. G. Schober, B. Keller, S. S. Schmucker, and C. P. Krauth, be a committee to prepare a Hymn-Book, Liturgy, and a collection of Prayers, in the English language, for the use of our Church, adhering particularly to the New York Hymn-Book, and German Liturgy of Pennsylvania, as their guides; and that they report thereon to the next General Synod.[43]

Two years later the committee reported to the General Synod assembled in Gettysburg.

The Committee appointed to prepare for publication a new and comprehensive selection of Hymns, for the use of our churches respectfully report, that they have devoted their most particular and prayerful attention to the important business assigned to them. They have produced all the most excellent and valuable hymn-books used by sister churches, and have also examined very many hymns found dispersed through the works of individual authors. They feel assured that the selection made will contain the major part of the best hymns extant in the English language. They have also, after mature consideration, constructed a new arrangement, which they deem decidedly more practical than any other which they have seen, and calculated to be more useful both to ministers and laymen. A general view of this arrangement they beg leave to submit to the consideration of the General Synod. The basis of the selection is the New York Hymn-Book, according to the instructors of this body; and the hymns selected from it, together with those intended to be added, will amount from eight to nine hundred.[44]

In 1828 the new hymnbook appeared as *Hymns, selected and original, for public and private worship*.[45] It was clearly more selected than original.[46] In addition to the reliance on the New York collection, this new hymnbook, which contained 766 hymns, "plainly purposed to embody the full scope of evangelical theology and every phase of evangelical experience."[47] Rationalism, which had characterized Quitman's hymnbook of 1814, was receding before a rising wave of revivalism, and this new volume was "in full sympathy with the new methods, appropriating many rude revival songs."[48]

The "new arrangement" for the hymnbook which the committee felt would be more practical and useful was a clearly Reformed pattern. Building on the arrangement of Quitman's *Collection of Hymns, and a Liturgy*, it was as far from a Lutheran pattern of hymnal organization as can be imagined. The ordering of hymns in this hymnbook was as follows:

> The Scriptures
> Being and Perfections of God
> Trinity
> Praise to God
> The Works of God
> Providence of God
> Fall and Depravity of Man
> Christ
> Names and Character of Christ
> Holy Spirit
> Gospel Call
> Penitence of the Awakened Sinner
> Supplication for the Divine Mercy
> Salvation Through Jesus Christ
> Christian Experience
> The Means of Grace
> Kingdom and Church of Christ
> Particular Occasions and Circumstances
> Death
> Resurrection
> Judgment
> Eternity
> Dismissions and Doxologies

Louis Benson, one of America's foremost hymnists, gives the following evaluation of Schmucker's efforts.

The textual treatment of the standard hymns is distressing, and as containing the authorized Hymnody of a historic Church, with its inherited standards of doctrine and churchmanship, the Hymns of 1828 seem singularly unworthy.[49]

E. E. Ryden comments regarding its theological and literary character that "*Hymns, selected and original* reveals many of the doctrinal aberrations that characterized the General Synod of that period. The book failed to reflect the true genius of the Lutheran Church. Moreover, the few Lutheran hymns it contained had been poorly translated."[50] A more positive review of Schmucker's hymnbook noted that there was little doubt that a new hymnbook had been needed.

> It was agreed on all hands, that Quitman's *Collection*, a book of an order superior to the one before in use, was wanting. That had been *sung out* long ago, and besides, it is manifestly deficient in several respects, which are at the present day, regarded as essential to Christian worship. Among other things, it wants variety and many of the most spiritual and highly poetical pieces in the language, are not to be found in it.[51]

That the deficiencies of the New York collection had, in the reviewer's evaluation, been more than corrected in Schmucker's hymnbook was evident from his concluding observation: "It breathes a most heavenly spirit, and we look upon its general success, as a good evidence of increasing spirituality among us."[52] The fact that Schmucker's *Hymns, selected and original* replaced a rationalistic hymnbook with one "thoroughly impregnated with Calvinistic and Arminian material of highly subjective character and with a dogmatic scheme which practically ignored the church year,"[53] did not prevent its enjoying a widespread popularity.

By 1835 it was reported that "the calls for the Hymn Book have, since the last meeting of this body, been more numerous than previously; and have especially extended to the Western and Southern portions of the Church."[54] Two years later the hymnbook was reported to have spread even more widely and was in use in the Middle Atlantic States, Ohio, New York, North and South Carolina, Kentucky, and Illinois.[55] The 1828 edition included the following interesting example:

How can a sinner know
His sins on earth forgiven?
How can my gracious Savior show
My name inscribed in heaven?
What we have *felt* and *seen*
With confidence we tell;
And publish to the sons of men
The signs infallible [Emphasis Bird's].

Bird suggests that "Our Methodist brethren have a right to believe and sing what they like; but we do object to anybody's palming off this sort of heresy upon us, in an official book of the Church, as Lutheran doctrine."

The Enlarged Edition of 1841, containing 965 hymns, carried on in the same vein and is devastatingly characterized by Bird as follows.

It is difficult to understand the principle on which this selection was made. The lowest taste and judgment seem to prevail; a reckless inconsistency, in doctrine, temper, style, and spirit, runs riot: Low Church and Broad Church, are mixed into an agreeable compound, representing some of the worst qualities of both, with not much of the redeeming features of either.[56]

By 1849 *Hymns, selected and original* had reached 56 editions or printings. Four years earlier the General Synod had appointed a committee headed by Dr. W. M. Reynolds[57] to revise the hymnbook.[58] At the 1848 meeting of the General Synod Reynolds presented a lengthy report suggesting many changes to strengthen its literary character and strongly encouraged the translating of more German hymns.[59] The new edition appeared in 1850 containing approximately 1,000 hymns. The overall result was a slight improvement, the number of revival songs being reduced and the chorale being given a place of somewhat greater prominence. A later edition in 1852 contained 1024 hymns, of which 35 were from the German.[60] It was a slight improvement, a small step forward toward a more genuinely Lutheran collection, due to the efforts of Reynolds, Baugher, and Schmucker who were responsible for this edition.

Typical of the impact of revivalism and the spread of the "new measures" in Lutheranism was the addition by mid-century to *Hymns, selected and original* of a section of hymns for "Revivals" and "Temperance." One such "Temperance" hymn was the following:

> Round the temp'rance standard rally,
>   All the friends of human kind;
> Snatch the devotees of folly,
>   Wretched, perishing and blind:
> Loudly tell them
> How they comfort now may find.
>
> Bear the blissful tidings onwards,
>   Bear them all the world around;
> Let the myriads thronging downwards
>   Hear the sweet and blissful sound,
> And, obeying,
> In the paths of peace be found.
>
> Plant the temp'rance standard firmly,
>   Round it live and round it die;
> Young and old defend it sternly,
>   Till we gain the victory,
> And all nations
> Hail the happy Jubilee.[61]

In "Praise for the increase of temperance," *Hymns, selected and original* offered the following:

> We praise Thee, Lord, if but one soul,
>   While the past year prolong'd it's flight,
> Turn'd shudd'ring from the pois'nous bowl,
>   To health and liberty and light.
>
> We praise thee—if one clouded home,
>   Where broken hearts despairing pin'd,
> Beheld the sire and husband come,
>   Erect, and in his perfect mind.

No more a weeping wife to mock,
　Till all her hopes in anguish end—
No more the trembling mind to shock,
　And sink the father in the fiend.

Still give us grace, Almighty King,
　Unwav'ring at our posts to stand;
Till grateful at thy shrine we bring
　The tribute of a ransom's land.[62]

Millenialism or chiliasm—referring to the period of 1000 years of Christ's reign apparently referred to in Rev. 20:1-7—was a part of the popular theology of frontier evangelism. Yet it is still surprising to find this hymn on "The Millennium" in a Lutheran hymnbook.

Look up, ye saints, with sweet surprise
　Behold the joyful coming day,
When Jesus shall descend the skies,
　And form a bright and dazzling ray.

Nations shall in a day be born,
　And swift, like doves, to Jesus fly:
The church shall know no cloud's return,
　Nor sorrows mixing with her joy.

The lion and the lamb shall feed
　Together, in his peaceful reign;
And Zion, blest with heav'nly bread,
　Of poverty no more complain.

The Jew, the Greek, the bond, the free,
　Shall boast their sep'rate rights no more,
But join in sweetest harmony,
　Their Lord, their Savior to adore.

Thus, till a thousand years be past,
　Shall holiness and peace prevail,
And ev'ry knee shall bow to Christ,
　And ev'ry tongue shall Jesus hail.

Then the redeem'd shall mount on high,
Where their deliv'ring Prince has gone;
And angels at his word shall fly,
To bless them with the conqu'ror's crown.[63]

Following the Civil War, the General Synod, greatly diminished by the formation of the General Synod of the South and the General Council, once more revised its hymnody. In 1871 it issued a Book of Worship[64] based on the 1852 edition of Hymns, selected and original. It was no significant improvement upon the earlier editions. The extent to which Hymns, selected and original in its various editions was used together with its general importance is ably summarized by Benson.

> The General Synod never at any time included all the synods or a majority of the Lutherans, but in the absence of any English hymn book put forth by the Pennsylvania Ministerium, its Hymns, selected and original, came the nearest to being the common hymnbook of English-speaking Lutherans. It came into use in probably not less than four-fifths of their congregations. Its successive editions mark the progress of the Anglicizing process, and cover a period in which the ways of surrounding denominations prevailed over Lutheran traditions.[65]

The common situation of the English Lutheran hymnbooks of the first half of the 19th century was that, judging by their content, they were something other than characteristically Lutheran. It was the fate of Kunze's A Hymn and Prayer-Book, relatively the most Lutheran of them all, to carry a decidedly Moravian flavor. Quitman's A Collection of Hymns, and a Liturgy was "a cross between high Arianism, and a mild loose form of cosmopolite old-style orthodoxy,"[66] while Hymns, selected and original of the General Synod, reflecting the looser confessional position of the time and the appropriation of the materials and methods of revivalism, presented "an agreeable mixture, in varying proportions, of Methodist and New School Presbyterianism, relieved by a gentle tincture of our faith."[67]

The *Evangelische Liedersammlung* of 1833

While the formation of the General Synod in 1820 did help to establish a broader base for a specific Lutheran identity than had previously been the case, even the General Synod recognized that "common hymnbooks"—developed for joint use by Lutheran and Reformed congregations—were widely used throughout its membership and would not easily be displaced. The plan for the formation of the General Synod stated specifically that

> The General Synod has the exclusive right with the concurrence of a majority of the particular Synods to introduce new books for general use in the public church service as well as to make improvement in the liturgy; but until this be done the hymn-books or collections of hymns now in use . . . shall continue in public use at pleasure.[88]

For more than the first decade of its existence, the General Synod was content to maintain the status quo and made no plans for the introduction of new hymnbooks. In 1827 when the matter was discussed at a meeting of the General Synod regarding "the publication of a new hymnbook in the German language which would be adapted to the use of Lutheran and Reformed congregations"[69] it was resolved by considering the financial implications and the possible disturbance to congregational worship that might result. The lack of any serious confessional concern regarding the use of such a book was apparent in their discussion. The resolution was not to recommend any action.[70] However, a few years later, the General Synod proceeded with plans for the publication of a new collection of German hymns and appointed a committee of J. G. Schmucker, F. Heyer, A. Lochman, E. L. Hazelius, S. S. Schmucker, D. F. Schaeffer, and J. G. Morris to prepare a new book.[71]

In 1833 it was reported to the General Synod that "the new collection of German songs considered by the previous synod and entrusted to the discretion of the committee is now in the press . . ."[72] The book appeared that same year as the *Evangelische Liedersammlung*,[73] published in Philadelphia and containing 415 hymns. It was clear that while a return to Muhlenberg's pioneering endeavor in Lutheran hymnody no longer reflected the spirit of the day, there was a certain nostalgic attachment to his work. The result was that the hymns of the *Evangelische Liedersammlung* were selected partly from the "old Pennsylvania hymnbook" of Muhlenberg and partly from the "common hymnbook." The fact that it returned, to some extent at least, for a portion of its hymnody to Muhlenberg's hymnbook and restored some of the excellent old hymns, made it, in Luther Reed's view, "a vast improvement upon the book of 1818 [1817]."[74] In fact it was no improvement at all over the "common hymnbook" of 1817. What was clearly evident was that there was need for a better hymnal.

The *Evangelische Liedersammlung* brought with it implications for the musical development of American Lutheran hymnody as well.

> Many hymns in the current hymnals have no melodies at all assigned to them, and others are so difficult that they could almost never be sung in the churches. Such hymns we have here omitted, and have added others set to easier melodies, also some to common English melodies.

The movement away from the hymnic heritage of the Lutheran Reformation and toward a more complete Anglicizing of the music of Lutheran congregation song in America was well under way.

But already in the third and fourth decade of the 19th century, a confessional revival, which involved not only those Lutherans who were already in America but a new wave of immigrants as well, sought to return Lutheranism in America to its roots in the 16th century. In the 300 years since the Reformation, the significant theological, liturgical, and hymnological heritage of the Lutheran Reformation had been vitiated by the inroads of Pietism, rationalism, and an amiable ecumenism that often resulted in the absorption of elements from the neighboring denominations in America that were inconsistent with its heritage. Part of the confessional revival included a return to a liturgical practice and a hymnody that reflected more adequately a Lutheran understanding of both. The hymnbooks and the hymnody of American Lutherans began a long, slow journey to its roots. From the viewpoint of the church's song, it was a revival long overdue.

Title page of *Geistliche Lieder* (1545), the so–called Babst hymnbook, "the finest hymnal of the Reformation period."

1. Th. 174.   904.   Ausz. 591.

1 Herzlich lieb hab ich dich, o HErr! ich
bitt, du wollst seyn von mir nicht
fern mit deiner hülf und gnaden : die
gantze welt mich erfreuet nicht, nach himmel und erden frag ich nicht, wenn ich
dich nur kann haben : und wenn mir
gleich mein hertz zerbricht, so bist du doch
mein' Zuversicht, mein Heil und meines
hertzens Trost, der mich durch sein blut
hat erlöf't. HErr JEsu Christ, mein
GOtt und HErr! mein GOtt und HErr!
in schanden laß mich nimmermehr.

2. Es ist ja, HErr, dein g'schenck und
gab mein leib, seel und all's, was ich hab
in diesem armen leben: damit ichs brauch
zum lobe dein, zum nutz und dienst des
nächsten mein, wollst mir dein' gnade geben! Behüt mich, HErr, vor falscher

lehr, des satans mord und lügen mehr:
in allem creutz erhalte mich, auf daß ich
trag geduldiglich. HErr JEsu Christ,
mein HErr und GOtt! mein HErr und
GOtt! tröst mir mein seel in todes-
noth.

3. Ach HErr! laß dein' lieb' engelein
am letzten end' die seele mein in Abra-
hams schooß tragen, den leib in sein'm
schlaff-kämmerlein gar sanft, ohn ein'ge
quaal und pein, ruhn bis am jüngsten ta-
ge: alsdenn vom tod erwecke mich,
daß meine augen sehen dich in aller
freud, o GOttes Sohn! mein Heiland
und Genaden-Thron. HERR JESU
CHrist, erhöre mich! erhöre mich! ich
will dich preisen ewiglich.

1. Th. 375.   905.   Ausz. 592.
Mel. Auf Triumph! es kommt die stunde, 2c. Oder:

Höchste

Erbauliche

Lieder-Samlung

Zum

Gottesdienſtlichen Gebrauch

in den

Vereinigten Evangeliſch Lutheriſchen

Gemeinen

in

Nord-America;

Geſamlet, eingerichtet und zum Druck be-
fördert durch die geſamten Glieder
des hieſigen

Vereinigten Evangeliſch Lutheriſchen

Ministeriums.

Erſte Auflage.

Germantaun,
Gedruckt bey Leibert und Billmeyer, 1786.

Title page of Muhlenberg's *Erbauliche Liedersammlung* (1786). Produced by the Pennsylvania Ministerium, it was the first official
Lutheran hymnbook in America.

Page from the *Choral–Buch fuer die Erbauliche Liedersammlung* (1813) showing melody with figured bass of the chorale "Ein feste Burg ist unser Gott."

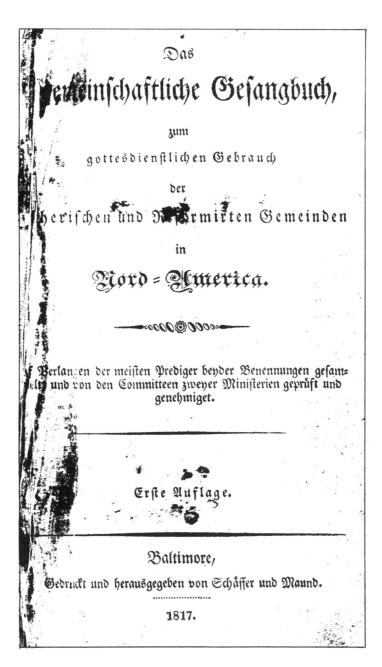

Das

Gemeinschaftliche Gesangbuch,

zum

gottesdienstlichen Gebrauch

der

Lutherischen und Reformirten Gemeinden

in

Nord = America.

●●○○○○◎○○○○●

Verlangen der meisten Prediger beyder Benennungen gesam=
melt und von den Committeen zweyer Ministerien geprüft und
genehmiget.

Erste Auflage.

Baltimore,

Gedruckt und herausgegeben von Schäffer und Maund.
....

1817.

Title page of *Das Gemeinschaftliche Gesangbuch* (1817), the
first of several "common hymnbooks" designed for use by
both Lutheran and Reformed congregations.

A COLLECTION

OF

H Y M N S,

AND

A LITURGY,

FOR THE USE OF

EVANGELICAL LUTHERAN CHURCHES;

TO WHICH ARE ADDED

PRAYERS

FOR FAMILIES AND INDIVIDUALS.

PUBLISHED BY ORDER

OF THE EVANGELICAL LUTHERAN SYNOD

OF THE STATE OF NEW YORK.

" I will pray with the spirit, and I will pray with the understanding also. I will sing with the spirit, and I will sing with the understanding also," 1 CoR. xiv.15.

PHILADELPHIA:
PRINTED AND SOLD BY G. & D. BILLMEYER.

1814.

Title page of Frederick Quitman's *A Collection of Hymns and a Liturgy* (1814), arguably one of the two poorest Lutheran hymnbooks ever produced in America.

HYMNS,

SELECTED AND ORIGINAL,

FOR

PRIVATE AND PUBLIC WORSHIP;

PUBLISHED BY THE

General Synod

FOR THE

EVANGELICAL LUTHERAN CHURCH.

THIRTY-SECOND EDITION.

(Third Edition with the Appendix.)

67792

BALTIMORE:

PUBLICATION ROOMS NO. 7 & LIBERTY STREET.

1843.

Title page of Samuel Simon Schmucker's *Hymns, selected and original* (1828) which reflected the effects of the movement of "American Lutheranism" and frontier revivalism.

CHURCH BOOK

FOR THE USE OF

EVANGELICAL LUTHERAN CONGREGATIONS.

———

BY AUTHORITY OF THE GENERAL COUNCIL OF THE EVANGELICAL
LUTHERAN CHURCH IN AMERICA.

———

PHILADELPHIA:
LUTHERAN BOOK STORE.

Title page of the General Council's *Church Book* (1868) which marked the beginning of a return to a more confessional hymnody among Lutherans in America.

Church Book,

FOR THE USE OF

Evangelical Lutheran Congregations.

BY AUTHORITY OF THE

GENERAL COUNCIL OF THE EVANGELICAL LUTHERAN CHURCH IN AMERICA.

With Music,

ARRANGED FOR THE USE OF CONGREGATIONS,

BY

HARRIET REYNOLDS KRAUTH.

PUBLISHED WITH THE RECOMMENDATION OF THE
GENERAL COUNCIL.

PHILADELPHIA:
GENERAL COUNCIL PUBLICATION BOARD.

Title page of the General Council's *Church Book with Music* (1872) for which Harriet Reynolds Krauth was the music editor.

Common Service Book

of the

Lutheran Church

Authorized by

The United Lutheran Church
in America

41809

Philadelphia

The Board of Publication of
The United Lutheran Church in America

Title page of the *Common Service Book of the Lutheran Church* (1917) which
appeared on the 400th anniversary of the Lutheran Reformation.

Service Book

and

Hymnal

Authorized by the Lutheran Churches

cooperating in

The Commission on the Liturgy and Hymnal

MUSIC EDITION

Title page of the *Service Book and Hymnal* (1958), the joint project of eight cooperating Lutheran church bodies.

Harriet Reynolds Krauth (1845–1925), music editor of the *Church Book with Music* (1872), the only woman to serve in such a capacity in American Lutheranism.

Samuel Simon Schmucker (1799–1873), leader of the movement for an "American Lutheranism," and largely responsible for the General Synod's *Hymns, selected and original* (1828).

Luther D. Reed (1873–1972), pioneer Lutheran leader in worship and liturgy and influential in the development of both the *Common Service Book* (1917) and the *Service Book and Hymnal* (1958).

Carl Ferdinand Wilhelm Walther (1811–1887), leader of the Saxon immigrants who came to America in 1839, and editor of the *Kirchengesangbuch fuer Evangelisch–Lutherische Gemeinden ungeaenderter Augsburgischer Confession* (1847).

Johann Andrew Augustus Grabau (1804–1879), leader of the Prussian Lutherans who emigrated to America in 1839, and editor of the *Evangelisch–Lutherisches Kirchen–Gesang–Buch* (1842).

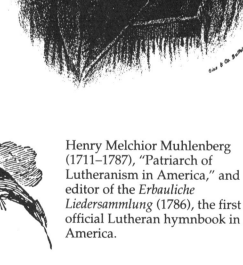

Henry Melchior Muhlenberg (1711–1787), "Patriarch of Lutheranism in America," and editor of the *Erbauliche Liedersammlung* (1786), the first official Lutheran hymnbook in America.

6

The Hymnody
of the 19th-Century
Scandinavian Immigrants

The immigrants from the Scandinavian countries of Denmark, Norway, Sweden, and Finland who came to America in the 1800s constituted the second-largest of the immigrant groups of Lutherans in the New World, second only to the Germans.[1] Their contribution to the church's song in America has been significant.

The Swedes

A small group of Swedish immigrants arrived in 1845 in the Mississippi Valley, settling in Jefferson County, Iowa, calling their community New Sweden. The first ordained Swedish pastor to arrive in the Midwest was Lars P. Esbjorn, a strong pietist, who, with 146 immigrants ultimately reached Andover, Illinois. He soon extended his field of labor to Moline, Rock Island, Galesburg, Princeton, Swedona, and other places in that area. Ultimately, the Swedish immigrants formed the Augustana Evangelical Lutheran Church in 1860.

The hymnody of the Swedish immigrants who first came to America was in the language of their homeland. The hymnbook favored by the founders of the Augustana Synod was the so-called Thomander-Wieselgren *Psalmbok* of 1849.[2] This book, published in Sweden, was a revision in the direction of a stricter orthodoxy by J. H. Thomander and P. Wieselgren of the famous hymnbook of Johan Olof

Wallin published in 1819. Wallin's hymnbook had been severely criticized in Sweden, especially by pietistic groups, who felt that it was influenced by the rationalism of the day and for a general disrespect for the classical orthodox tradition. C. J. F. Haeffner's *Svensk Choralbok* (1820–21), for example, intend-ed to accompany Wallin's 1819 *Psalmbok*, had replaced the earlier rhythmic form of the Reformation melodies. Instead "the tunes are harmonized in strict four-part choral style, triple and irregular meters are almost entirely deleted, the modal character of most tunes is lost, and the more florid, melis-matic phrases of the melodies are severely truncated." As a result there were several attempts to revise or replace Wallin's book, the most successful of them being the revision in the direction of orthodoxy by Thomander and Wieselgren.

Although ultimately rejected in Sweden, the Thoman-der-Wieselgren *Psalmbok* became the official Swedish-lan-guage hymnbook of the Augustana Synod in North Amer-ica. In a pamphlet entitled "Advice to Emigrants" by Erland Carlsson, the author recommended that emigrants to Amer-ica bring with them their copies of the Thomander-Wieselgren hymnbook, even though it had found little favor in Sweden. The Augustana Synod resolved to instruct the Swedish Evangelical Lutheran Publication Society to print this edition of the Swedish Psalmbook, and in 1865 it was reported off the press, and the following year bound copies were available for congregational use in America. A second edition was printed in 1871 edited by Jonas Engberg of Immanuel Church of Chicago, Illinois. The second edition was hardly off the press, however, when the printing plates and the remaining copies were destroyed in the Great Chicago Fire of October, 1871. Other arrangements had to be made for supplying copies, but it was not until 1877 that a ready supply was once again available.

The influence of the pietist movement on the congregational song in the churches of 19th-century Sweden was also carried to the immigrant churches in America. In Sweden, about mid-19th century, a wave of revivalism swept the country. The "new evangelicalism," as it was called, was led by the famous lay preacher Carl Rosenius. Rosenius and his followers, among them Karolina Sandell Berg,[4] the "Fanny Crosby of Sweden," and Askar Ahnfelt, a "spiritual troubador" who traveled through Scandinavia singing to the accompaniment of a guitar, wrote many texts and tunes of a lighter, more subjective character which became very popular, and were published in ever-enlarging collections called *Andeliga Sanger* (Spiritual Songs).

This more subjective song was carried to America by the Swedish immigrants. The first Swedish songbook to be printed in America was the *Femtio Andeliga Sanger*[5] (Fifty Spiritual Songs) issued in 1856 by Tuve Nilsson Hasselquist (1816–91)[6] and based largely on the work of Askar Ahnfelt, perhaps the chief popularizer of the more subjective songs of the revival. In 1860 the *Hemlandssanger*, a popular collection of similar songs, was published by Jonas Engberg on his own initiative.[7] It contained 240 songs of the pietistic revival movement and was widely used. A second enlarged edition followed in 1866 containing 413 hymns.

There were those who favored revision of the more conservative Psalmbook and those who favored publication of a separate songbook that might incorporate more of the subjective evangelical hymns. The Rev. Hasselquist posed the question in the discussion that preceded the decision to produce a separate book.

> We need to discuss the question what difference there is between a psalmbook and a songbook. I think there is such a difference and that they should not be combined in one book unless the songbook were so small that it could form an appendix to the former.[8]

This was finally resolved in 1877 when the Augustana Synod determined to issue a separate publication. Because Engberg's collection had been so well received, permission was received to appropriate this title for the authorized separate publication which appeared in 1892. This new *Hemlandssanger* contained 500 songs, of which 98 were by Karolina

Sandell Berg, together with others by Rosenius, Ahnfelt, and similar writers of the pietistic evangelical revival movement.

A hymnbook in English was contemplated as early as 1887, but nothing was done until 1895 when the synod instructed the theological faculty at the Augustana Seminary in Rock Island, Illinois, to prepare such a book. An English text edition of 355 hymns was submitted, approved, and it appeared in 1899 as the *Hymnal and Order of Service for Churches and Sunday Schools.*[9] A complete music edition appeared two years later in 1901 under the editorship of Dr. Alfred Ostrom, who was also largely responsible for the musical settings.[10] Of the hymns in this collection about 143 are from the Swedish.

Prepared as only a temporary arrangement until a more adequate book could be prepared, the 1901 hymnbook remained in use until 1925 when the *Hymnal and Order of Service*[11] was published. Editors of this new book were Dr. C. W. Foss and Rev. I. O. Nothstein; the choice of tunes and the editing of the music for the liturgy was entrusted to Rev. E. E. Ryden.[12] Of its 663 hymns, about 73 are translations from the Swedish. This hymnal exhibits the conflict between those who attempted to preserve the historic heritage of the church's song and those who sought to extend the use of the subjective songs of the evangelical revival.

The Swedish church in America, untroubled by divisive schism of one kind or another, but pressured for a greater use of subjective revival songs in their worship, retained only a handful of the hymns of the 16th-century Reformation. By the middle of the 20th century, the Augustana Evangelical Lutheran Church would be cooperating, together with other Lutheran groups, in the production of the *Service Book and Hymnal* of 1958.

The Danes

The history of the Danes and the Norwegians—in

hymnody as in politics—were closely linked until Norway became an independent nation in 1814. Mandus Egge remarks that the history of Norway apart from that of Denmark did not begin until the middle of the 19th century.[13] From Thomisson's *Den danske Psalmebog* of 1596 to the beginning of the 19th century, the same hymnbooks and chorale books were used in both countries. Thomisson's *Psalmebog*—whose 203 melodies were drawn primarily from German chorale tunes and Danish folksongs—served for 150 years, when it was replaced in 1699 by a new book by Thomas Kingo, Denmark's first great hymn writer often referred to as the "singer of orthodoxy."

By the mid-1700s the results of the so-called "reform" movement, which favored the abandonment of the original rhythmic forms of the chorale melodies in favor of the even-note, isometric form, were clearly evident in F. C. Breitendich's *Fuldstaendig Choral-Bog* of 1764. This development was furthered in such collections as the *Kirche-Melodierne* of 1781, the Niels Schiorring's *Choral-Bog* of 1783, and Harnock Zinck's *Koral-Melodier* of 1801. It was this which formed the background for the Danish and Norwegian immigrants to America in the 19th century.

The development of hymnody among the Danish and Norwegian immigrants followed much the same pattern as that of the Swedish immigrants. In the case of the Danes, however, the immigrants had no help at all from the Church of Denmark. As Jenson remarked, "Not a single theologian from Denmark came over to help them. They were completely on their own."[14] In addition, the numbers of Danish immigrants and their general resources were small. The first congregation organized by the Danes was apparently in Indianapolis, Indiana in 1868, while the first Danish church body to be organized was the Danish Evangelical Lutheran Church established in 1874.

Danish immigrants undoubtedly brought with them such collections as those by Kingo, Balle, and the Guldberg-Harboe *Psalmebog*. For a variety of reasons they were unable to produce any hymnbooks of their own in the

Danish language. Liemohn notes that "the *Salmebog for Kirche og Hjem*, published in Denmark in 1897, has been the accepted hymnal for churches in America using the Danish language."[15] The 1892 publication of *Sangeren*, a collection of "gospel songs," also "became tremendously popular in the Blair [Nebraska] Church and later in the UDELC. It was published in many editions and was used at all special meetings of the church and in Sunday schools."[16]

In addition to reprint editions of the *Salmebog for Kirke og Hjem*, the *Roskilde Konventssalmebog* of 1855 was also used by some Danish congregations.[17] Both of these collections are important in the history of Danish hymnody. The *Roskilde Konventssalmebog* of 1855 was the work of Bernard Severin Ingemann (1789–1862). The *Salmebog for Kirke og Hjem* of 1897 was dominated by the hymnody of Nicolai Grundtvig, Thomas Kingo, Hans Brorson, and Ingemann. This latter volume particularly represented a developing churchly character in Danish hymnody. These two volumes, then, largely determined the shape of Danish Lutheran hymnody in America.

In 1919 S. D. Rodholm published *Hymns of the North*, a small volume of 26 translated Danish hymns, which became quite popular so that by 1922 a total of three revised and enlarged editions had appeared.[18] By 1922 a committee was appointed "to compile an English hymnbook with hymns translated from Danish, and other English hymns loved by the church."[19] P. C. Paulsen and E. S. Rosenberg were appointed to the committee, Paulsen soon becoming the leader, translating many of the Danish hymns himself. Other members of the committee included J. C. Aaberg, Ingvard Andersen, and A. Th. Dorf. This English hymnal appeared in 1927 as the *Hymnal for Church and Home.*[20] The hymnbook was in effect a joint product of the Danish Lutheran Church and the United Danish Lutheran Church. It went through several editions, the third edition of 1938 containing an additional 150 hymns.

A *Junior Hymnal* appeared in 1932 and again in 1944, revised and enlarged. Commenting on both the *Hymnal for*

Church and Home and the *Junior Hymnal,* Jensen summarizes their significance.

> Both of these hymnals were sponsored by the two synods of Danish background. They contained translations into English of many of the best-loved Danish hymns. Thus the second- and third-generation Danish American could sing the hymns his parents loved, the melodies of which evoked the memory of the faith of his fathers, in a language that he himself could understand.

The Norwegians

As Norwegian immigrants came to America in the 1830s and settled in the upper mid-West, in a fashion similar to most immigrant groups, they brought with them to America the hymnals which they had used in their homeland. Liemohn mentions, among others, the Balle hymnbook of 1797, Guldberg's hymnbook of 1778, Thomas Kingo's book of 1819, and the Harboe-Guldberg book of 1823—these from the Danish period, and, from Norway's own great hymnist, Magnus Lanstad's *Psalmebog* of 1869 (a revised edition of his *Kirche-Psalmebog et Udkast* of 1861), as among the hymnbooks used by the Norwegian immigrants.[21] Landstad's *Psalmebog* of 1869 was extremely popular and was in use in over two-thirds of the parishes of Norway by 1870. Reprints of the Guldberg hymnbook were published in 1854, one at Norway, Illinois, by Ole Andreasen, and the other by the Scandinavian Press Association at Inmansville, Wisconsin. Some years later, in 1893, the United Norwegian Lutheran Church and the Hauge Lutheran Synod joined together in the publication of Landstad's hymnbook to which they added 96 hymns.

Of particular importance to the Norwegian immigrants was the influence of Magnus Landstad's *Psalmebog* of 1869 together with the *Koralbog* of Ludwig Lindemann. These two men had collaborated in what Liemohn considers Norway's "first satisfactory hymnal."[22] Ludwig Lindemann had inherited a melodic tradition based on the chorale book of his father Ole Lindemann published in 1838.

The publication of Ole Lindemann's *Choralebog* in 1835 with its largely even-note melodies, set off a controversy regarding the form of the melodies that lasted for almost 50 years. Characteristic of Ole Lindemann's chorale book are the use of a different harmonization for repeated phrases and the "pages and pages of half notes, interrupted only occasionally by a quarter note."[23] Lindemann's book represented a departure from the original Reformation melodies as congregations had sung them "until the last century's desire to change, lacking in taste and churchly sense or depth, particularly to remove their rhythmic features, handling them in such a manner as to render most of them unrecognizable . . ."[24] Among those who advocated a return to the original rhythmic form of the Reformation chorales were J. D. Behrens, Erik Hoff, and O. Winter-Hjelm, author of *37 aeldre Salmemelodier*, an important tract on the Lutheran chorale. Opposing them was Ludvig Lindemann, the so-called "Romanticist of Norwegian church music."

Ludvig Lindemann's chorale book of 1871 sought to correct the problems of his father's book. He substituted the quarter note for the half note as the basic unit of meter, syncopation in the early melodies was largely removed, substituting ♩ ♩♩ for ♩♩ ♩ . In an attempt to inject a more vigorous element into these melodies, he often substituted ♩. ♪ for ♩ ♩ . Whatever his views on the rhythmic chorale, Ludvig Lindemann had a profound influence on the course of congregational singing among Norwegian Lutherans, both in Norway and among the immigrants in America.

The two streams of influence that dominated 19th-century Norwegian Lutheranism and that were transplanted to America were the Haugean spirit of a deeply personal piety with an emphasis on lay activity following Hans Hauge and the emphasis on Biblical doctrine and a confessional Lutheranism that reflected the more traditional stance of the church in Norway.

The first hymnbook to be published in the Norwegian language in America was the work of Ulrik Koren, president of the Norwegian Synod, published in 1874. Its 515 hymns included 115 of Landstad's, together with 27 original texts and 21 translations by Koren. The earliest English hymnbook published by the Norwegians in America was the *Hymnbook for the use of Evangelical Lutheran Schools and Congregations*,[25] published in Decorah, Iowa, in 1879, and edited by Prof. August Crull, at that time a teacher at Concordia College, Fort Wayne, Indiana. This hymnbook, containing 130 hymns and 10 doxologies, was highly praised by C. F. W. Walther[26] and was undoubtedly used in some of the congregations of the Missouri Synod. Two other early English collections were the *Church and Sunday School Hymnal*[27] of the United Norwegian Lutheran Church and the *Christian Hymns for Church, School and Home*[28] of the Norwegian Synod.

The English hymnbook of major significance from the Norwegian heritage is *The Lutheran Hymnary* of 1913. The story of that book is told in a later chapter.

The Finns

While Finns had been represented among the first Swedish immigrants to America in the 17th century,[29] the migration of larger numbers of immigrants from Finland came in the latter half of the 19th century. They settled largely in the northern states with concentration in Minnesota, Northern Michigan, and Canada. The Finnish Evangelical Lutheran Church of America, generally known as the Suomi Synod, was organized in 1890.

The first Finnish-language hymnbook used in America was the *Suomalainen Virsikirja* (Finnish Hymnbook), published in Helsinki in 1886, which the Finnish immigrants brought with them from their homeland. In 1909 this collection was reprinted in America by the Finnish Lutheran

Book Concern in Hancock, Michigan. They also used a chorale book, the *Koraalikirja*, which had been published in Helsinki in 1909. In 1925 *Siionin Lauluja* (Songs of Zion), a collection largely in Finnish but with the addition of some English-language hymns, was also published in Hancock, Michigan, as was a Sunday School collection, *Pyhakoulun Laulukirja*, which contained both Finnish- and English-language hymns.

After 1930, by authorization of the Synod, the Finns, who had always had a close affinity with the Swedes, used the Augustana Synod's *The Hymnal and Order of Service* of 1925 together with an English translation of the Finnish liturgy that had been published in Hancock, Michigan. The Suomi Synod had always been a rather small group, and in 1962 it merged with several other Lutheran groups to form the Lutheran Church in America.

7

The Movement Toward a More Confessional Hymnody

The hymnals and hymnody of American Lutheranism's early years were rooted in the Pietistic hymnals of 18th-century Germany. Pietism, while initially retaining a link with the confessional hymnody of the Reformation's early years, tended to find the personal, subjective, or even mystical hymns of such 17th-century writers as Paul Gerhardt, Johann Franck, or Johann Scheffler more compatible with its outlook than the more objective, didactic, or narrative hymnody of such 16th-century writers as Martin Luther, Paul Speratus, or Justus Jonas. Pietism stressed the subjective aspects of human religious experience and urged a moralism apart from the means of grace. The Reformation accent on objective justification, so strong an emphasis in the Lutheran hymns of the 16th century, was slowly replaced by an increasingly subjective emphasis on moral perfection.

Henry Melchior Muhlenberg exemplified this point of view. Even this great shaper of American Lutheranism found it difficult to see the vigor and relevance of the hymnic heritage of the 16th century, considering many of the great ancient and medieval texts to be "harsh in construction, rhyme, etc." Some he retained, he suggested, because they were "familiar to all Lutherans from childhood," others because they were "nevertheless orthodox."

With the rise of rationalism and unionism at the beginning of the 19th century, even Muhlenberg's tenuous link with 16th-century hymnody gave way before forces which sought to rework the church's song. Rationalism worked to bring hymnody in line with human reason; unionism effectively diluted it in order to facilitate organizational unity. Increasing contact with surrounding denominations in America, particularly as the church moved westward along the frontier, did little to reinforce the use of distinctive Lutheran worship practices and hymnody. While rationalism, unionism, and revivalism were, for a time, successful, they ultimately gave way before a new movement emphasizing the necessity of a truly confessional hymnody rooted in Lutheranism's own heritage.

Claus Harms (1778–1855) in his new set of "Ninety-five Theses" published in Germany in 1817 in connection with the 300th anniversary of the Reformation was simply reminding the church of what had already occurred when he remarked that "the acceptance of reason in the Lutheran Church would cause only confusion and destruction . . . in the authorized and accepted agendas, hymnals, and catechisms."[1] As this revival of confessional interest was related to the church's hymnody, it manifested itself primarily in two ways. It sought

1) to restore to the church the original and unaltered texts of the historic Kernlieder of the Reformation period; and

2) to recapture the musical vitality of that age through the restoration of the original rhythmic forms of the chorale melodies, the loss of which was viewed as the chief reason for the decline in congregational singing.

That congregational singing had suffered a sever decline since the time of the Reformation is evident from any number of reports. The eminent English historian Charles Burney (1726–1814) reported on his experience at a Lutheran church in Bremen in the late 18th century:

> I visited the Thumkirche or cathedral, belonging to the
> Lutherans, where I found the congregation singing a dismal
> melody, without the organ. When this was ended, the organist
> gave out a hymn tune, in the true dragging style of Sternhold
> and Hopkins. . . . The interludes between each line of the hymn
> were always the same, and of the following kind: [musical
> example] After hearing this tune, and these interludes,
> repeated ten or twelve times, I went to see the town, and
> returning to the cathedral, two hours after, I still found the
> people singing all in unison, and as loud as they could, the same
> tune, to the same accompaniment. I went to the post-office, to
> make dispositions for my departure; and, rather from curiosity
> than the love of such music, I returned once more to this church,
> and, to my great astonishment, still found them, vocally and
> organically performing the same ditty, the duration of which
> seems to have exceeded that of a Scots Hymn, in the time of
> Charles I.[2]

In 1847 the following description of congregational singing
in Germany was typical of the experience of most of the
immigrants who were to come to America in the 1830s and
1840s. It clearly shows the depths to which congregational
singing had fallen.

> Each syllable is sung without distinction for a period of about
> four beats; on the last syllable of each line or at the end of the
> melodic phrase there follows a long fermata lasting 8–12 beats,
> the part of which is incorporated in a more or less intricate
> organ interlude. So all the melodies follow one line after the
> other in this repetitious manner, whether sad or joyous,
> mournful or exultant, all performed in a creeping, dragging
> fashion. The hymns of Luther have had their wings clipped
> and have put on the straightjacket of 4/4 time. And so it came
> about the more inflexible the singing of the chorale was, the
> more solemn it was thought to be.[3]

It was to the revival of a more vigorous congregational song
from the sad situation in which congregational singing
found itself that the confessional revival also addressed

123

itself.

The movement for confessional revival, begun in Germany as a theological concern, had an immediate effect upon the course of Lutheran hymnody, both in Germany and America. The impetus for the confessional revival in America came from two quite different groups. The first was that group of Lutherans who were the descendants of those who had come to America in the 1700s, the spiritual descendants of Muhlenberg. The second group consisted of several immigrant groups that had come to America beginning in the late 1830s: the Prussians, the Saxons, and the Bavarians.

The rise of Lutheran confessionalism in 19th-century America expressed itself in several ways: the gradual rejection of the rationalism of the early years of the century; the rejection of the movement of "American Lutheranism" led by S. S. Schmucker in the middle years of the century that sought to recast historic Lutheranism in a radically different confessional mold in order, so it thought, to better accommodate Lutheranism to the American situation; and in moves to form new groupings of more confessionally inclined Lutherans. The hymnals of the Lutheran groups in America clearly reflect this developing awareness of the need to recapture the confessional heritage of the hymnody of the early Reformation.

While the first Lutheran groups in America developed their concern for a confessional hymnody somewhat more slowly, the immigrant groups that came to America in the late 1830s came irrevocably committed to a strict confessional concern from the very first. While remaining largely aloof from other Lutherans, these new immigrant groups—the Prussians under Grabau, the Saxons under Walther, and the Bavarians sent to America by Wilhelm Loehe—acted as a leaven in encouraging the confessional movement among other Lutheran groups. The confessional concern of these immigrant groups was demonstrably evident in the hymnody they espoused and fostered.

Grabau's *Evangelisch-Lutherisches Kirchengesangbuch* of 1842

The year 1839 saw the emigration to America of two groups of German Lutherans whose coming was to herald a new concern for confessional hymnody. The first group to arrive was the Saxons who arrived in St. Louis in the first days of 1839. The second, and the first to produce a hymnbook, was a group of Prussians who arrived in America on July 1839, some six months after the Saxons, under the leadership of Rev. Johann Andrew Augustus Grabau (1804–1879) of Erfurt.[4]

J. A. A. Grabau was a pastor at Erfurt, Germany, who had resisted the imposition of a uniform liturgy, which he considered Reformed in character, and for which action he was twice imprisoned. Eventually he emigrated to America with members of congregations from Erfurt, Magdeburg, and elsewhere, arriving in America in the early days of 1839. About 1,000 in number, the Prussians settled in and near Buffalo in Western New York—which subsequently became the headquarters of the Buffalo Synod—and in Milwaukee, Wisconsin. They had left Prussia because of the efforts to unite Lutherans and Reformed churches into the Prussian Union. When a royal decree in 1830 abolished the old church books and sought to impose a uniform liturgy, many of the Prussians decided it was time to leave their homeland. A second major Prussian migration occurred in 1843 and brought 1600 more Lutherans to Western New York and Wisconsin where they placed themselves under Grabau's supervision.[5]

The Prussians under Grabau, like the Saxons under C. F. W. Walther, were a strongly confessional Lutheran group, and for a short time the possibility seemed to exist that this common bond would help to unite the Prussians, the

Saxons, and the emissaries of Wilhelm Loehe in Michigan and Indiana. However, a Pastoral Letter (*Hirtenbrief*), written by Grabau in 1840 and expressing a view of the church and ministry that the Saxons could not accept, set off a theological controversy between the Missouri Synod and the Buffalo Synod that continued for the greater part of the 19th century.

In the developing stages of this controversy with the Saxon immigrants over the theology set forth in his *Hirtenbrief*, Grabau was at work on a hymnbook that would serve the needs of the small number of congregations under his leadership. Grabau's work on this hymnbook even delayed his preparation for the ensuing controversy with the Saxons.[6] In 1842 Grabau published for the congregations under his leadership the *Evangelisch-Lutherisches Kirchengesangbuch*[7] containing 491 hymns together with a selection of prayers, collects, and various liturgical formulations. The committee that prepared the hymnbook consisted of Grabau, the editor, E. Krieg, and W. Hachemann, all from the congregation at Buffalo, New York.[8] While originally the product of a single congregation, it was later introduced into all the congregations of the Buffalo Synod following the formation of that synod in 1845. It was undoubtedly the most remarkable hymnbook that had yet appeared on the American continent.

Grabau utilized 33 old Lutheran hymn-books and agendas in compiling his hymnbook, most important of which was a "Lutheri Gesangbuch mit einem zweiten Theile vermehrt, Leipzig 1559 u. 1561."[9] This collection was a later reprint of Valentin Babst's hymnal of 1545, the last hymnal for which Martin Luther had written a preface and which was considered the most representative Lutheran hymnbook of the latter half of the 16th century.[10] This return to the Babst hymnbook was a harbinger of better things to come for American Lutheran hymnody. More than half of the hymns from the Babst 1545 hymnbook are found in Grabau's collection, including even some of the Latin hymns that were reproduced by Grabau in the Latin language.

Of the 491 hymns in the first edition of the *Evan-gelisch-Lutherisches Kirchen-Gesang-Buch*, approximately 40 were Latin hymns, printed in Latin. Grabau quoted Luther's words from the Babst hymnal as justification for this practice.

> Concerning the retention of the pure, old Latin hymns, Dr. Luther says in his hymnbook at No. 52: Dies est laetitiae: "We also have included these old hymns as a testimony of those devout Christians who lived before us in the darkness of false doctrine. So that one can easily see that at all times there were those who knew Christ aright and were marvelously kept in this same knowledge through God's grace."[11]

Grabau specifically points out that his concern was for the restoration of the "original readings"[12] (*die urspruengliche Lesart*) of the old Lutheran hymns, readings that had been corrupted in the intervening centuries. Grabau's reliance on the Babst hymnbook is also evident in that the prayers, collects, and other liturgical formulations were spaced throughout the hymnbook, being placed with the season of the church year to which they were related, rather than in an appendix at the back of the book, the more common practice of the time. The hymns were arranged according to the church year. As a repristination of 16th-century Lutheran hymnody, Grabau's hymnbook was the most Lutheran yet produced in America.

Seven editions of this hymnbook appeared during the later 19th century, Grabau personally supervising and carrying out the editing and correcting of the first five editions.[13] In the Preface to the fourth edition, which appeared in 1864/65, Grabau insisted that the Latin hymns continue to be included. But following Grabau's death in 1879 the Latin hymns were finally dropped. With the organization of the Buffalo Synod in 1845, Grabau's hymnbook was officially adopted and introduced into all its congregations. The congregations of the Buffalo Synod remained strict in doctrine and practice even though they remained a relatively small body within American

Lutheranism.

The Buffalo Synod's continuing concern for a confessional hymnody rooted in the Lutheran Reformation, is reflected in the following passage from its official church paper at the beginning of the 20th century.

> . . . the church song in its true and pure character is a gift with which the church of the Reformation has been highly blessed, and from which we have received and possess the very best. This treasury of the old Lutheran, classical church songs is what we have available in our church hymnbook in a striking selection which we have placed into the hands of our congregations and Christians.[14]

C. F. W. Walther's *Kirchengesangbuch* of 1847

While Grabau's Buffalo Synod remained a relatively small group within American Lutheranism, the Saxon immigrant group that arrived in St. Louis, Missouri in 1839, the same year as Grabau's Prussian immigrant group arrived in America, was to become one of the largest and most influential of American Lutheran bodies. Early in 1839 just over 600 Saxons arrived at St. Louis, soon to be followed by another 100 Saxons who had come through New York, and finally another 125 Saxons who arrived at the end of the year, coming through New Orleans. The leader of the Saxons, Rev. Martin Stephan, was almost immediately deposed as the result of a number of unfortunate circumstances, and the young pastor Carl Ferdinand Wilhelm Walther (1811–87) was thrust into the position of leadership.

Walther, barely 30 years old when he assumed leadership of the Saxon immigrants, was to play a crucial role in sounding the note for a more truly confessional Lutheran hymnody among American Lutherans.[15] Faced by a confusing array of hymnals in use among the Saxons,[16]

Walther brought to the attention of his congregation in St. Louis the need for a hymnal that could serve all confessional Lutheran groups.[17] In November 1845 the congregation resolved to proceed with plans for a new hymnal, and in August 1847 the hymnbook was introduced for use as the *Kirchengesangbuch fuer Evangelisch-Lutherische Gemeinden ungeaenderter Augsburgischer Confession.*[18] It contained 437 hymns together with a selection of prayers, antiphons, the Preface, Luther's Small Catechism, and the Augsburg Confession. The book was compiled by "several Lutheran pastors in Missouri,"[19] although it is clear that Walther himself took the leading part.[20]

The criteria that determined the selection of the hymns was described as follows.

In the selection of the adopted hymns the chief consideration was that they be pure in doctrine; that they have found almost universal acceptance within the orthodox German Lutheran Church and have thus received the almost universal testimony that they have come forth from the true spirit [of Lutheranism]; that they express not so much the changing circumstances of individual persons but rather contain the language of the whole church, because the book is to be used primarily in public worship; and finally that they, though bearing the imprint of Christian simplicity, be not merely rhymed prose but the creation of a truly Christian poetry.[21]

The significance of this hymnbook, emerging from the confessional revival and hymnological renaissance of the 19th century, was found in its stress on an evangelically orthodox hymnody, in its concern for a return to the normative core of 16th-century Lutheran hymns, and in the vigorous promotion throughout the Missouri Synod encouraging a return to the singing of the original rhythmic form of the chorale melodies.[22]

Walther's *Kirchengesangbuch,* begun as a project of the St. Louis congregation which he served, remained the property of the congregation until 1862 when the hymnbook was officially transferred to the parent church body.[23] It remained virtually without change throughout the entire period of its use. The only changes were the addition of six hymns with the 1857 printing, and the addition of a supplement of 41 more hymns in 1917. The concern of Walther, together with other leaders of the Missouri Synod, for a confessionally orthodox Lutheran hymnody is evident from the very first in the unusual amount of space given to this matter in the official journals and church papers at that time.[24] In addition, Walther's interest in music—he had seriously considered a career in music as a youth[25]—helped to direct the musical aspects of the Missouri Synod's hymnody into a path that reflected more closely its Reformation heritage.

From the earliest years, the two motifs of Missouri Synod hymnody were an evangelical concern for a confessionally orthodox hymnody coupled with a vital concern for the rhythmic form of the chorale melody. These two motifs consistently appear as the Missouri Synod defended its own confessional position against what it often considered the more lax position of other Lutherans, as it offered criticism of hymnals of other Lutheran groups, and as it attempted to chart a course in the transition to an English language hymnody. On the one hand, these concerns often prevented the Missouri Synod from cooperating or participating in common hymnological endeavors with other Lutherans who, they felt, did not share their strong convictions in matters of hymnody.[26] On the other hand, these concerns for congregational song preserved for American Lutheranism the heritage of Reformation hymnody, both texts and melodies, in a way that did not find similar expression among any other Lutheran bodies.

The importance of such a confessionally orthodox hymnody for the church, as well as a keen insight into the function of hymnody in worship, was clearly voiced by Walther in 1885 as he reviewed the newly published concordance[27] for the *Kirchengesangbuch* in *Der Lutheraner*.

In a proper and pure public service of worship it is not only fitting and necessary that the preacher preach only God's pure Word, but also that the congregation sing only pure hymns. This latter point is so necessary and is without doubt a matter of the greatest importance: that the preacher choose good hymns, and allow them to be sung, which properly prepares for the hearing of the Word of God and best serve to preserve and seal the Word already heard.[28]

The matter of singing the chorales in their newly recovered original rhythmic form presented another challenge. The congregations had to learn the new forms of the tunes; and the older books which had been used by organists and leaders of congregational song would no longer suffice because they followed the old isometric melodic forms. Two kinds of books needed to be made available to fill these needs: melody books for the congregation and chorale books for the organists.

Melody books (*Melodienbuecher*) were not uncommon in Germany of the mid-19th century. Friedrich Layriz, whose influence on the music of the Missouri Synod would be a profound one, had published several melody books as early as 1839.[29] These books, usually containing only the melody line without words, reprinted in a variety of editions in America, were used to familiarize the congregation with the new forms of the tunes. In Walther's St. Louis congregation, for example, regular practice sessions were held to learn the old church melodies.[30]

While the teaching of the rhythmic form of the chorale to the congregation was an immediate necessity, the problem of a *Choralbuch* for the organist was not so pressing. The first edition of Layriz' *Kern des deutschen Kirchengesangs*,[31] which appeared in 1844 and contained 200 four-part settings of the Lutheran chorale, apparently served to introduce the German immigrants to this material. It was the second edition of Layriz' collection, published in 1849, that served as the basic *Choralbuch* for this group for the next 15 years or so. In 1863 a new selection from Layriz' second edition was published as the *Evangelisch-Lutherisches Choralbuch fuer Kirche und Haus*[32] and was to serve until the late 1880s. In

1886 a new book for the organist was published as the *Choralbuch*,[33] largely the work of Heinrich F. Hoelter (1846–1916); two years later in 1888 there appeared the *Mehrstimmiges Choralbuch*,[34] the work of Karl Brauer (1831–1907).[35] These two chorale books, which took advantage of the new musicological research and publications of such men as Schoeberlein, Winterfeld, Zahn, and Layriz, continued to serve those congregations that conducted services in German far into the 20th century, by which time the transition into the English language was well under way for the Missouri Synod.

The Bavarians in Michigan and the Iowa Synod

The third immigrant group was the Bavarians, a group of approximately 90 people who set sail from Germany in May 1845, sent by Wilhelm Loehe of Neuendettelsau, to establish settlements in the Saginaw Valley of Michigan. They came to New York, by steamer up the Hudson River to Albany, by train to Buffalo, from there by boat to Detroit, and finally overland through the forest to the fertile Saginaw Valley where they established a series of settlements. They called their settlements Frankenmuth (Courage of the Franks or Bavarians), Frankenhilf (Help of the Franks), Frankenlust (Joy of the Franks), and Frankentrost (Consolation of the Franks). Their leader was the Rev. Friedrich Craemer (1812–91).

Attracted to Loehe by an appeal for help from Friedrich Wynecken, Craemer led his group to the wilds of northern Michigan where they established a mission colony that they hoped could serve the scattered Lutherans on the frontier as well as the American Indians who populated the area. Craemer had been ordained by Theodor Kliefoth, a leader in the confessional movement and in the movement for liturgical reform in Germany. Loehe, who was considered to be the most influential figure in 19th-century German liturgical renewal,[36] had prepared an agenda for "Christian Congregations of the Lutheran Confession" with the German Lutheran congregations in America specifically in mind, dedicated to Friedrich Wyneken of Fort Wayne, Indiana.[37] The services of the Bavarian communities included the weekly celebration of holy communion, Sunday afternoon catechization services, brief morning and evening services each day, summer and winter, and observation of the minor liturgical festivals on the appropriate day.[38]

While neither the Bavarians nor the Iowa Synod ever produced a German hymnal, both groups were important forces in the battle for a more confessional Lutheranism in America. The men whom Loehe sent to America in the 1840s soon established close contact with the Saxon immigrants. A number of them helped to form the Lutheran Church—Missouri Synod in 1847. However, a breach soon developed between Loehe and the Missourians. Although the visit of C. F. W. Walther and Friedrich Wyneken to Germany in 1851 seemed temporarily to have healed the division, a visit by Grabau to Loehe two years later seems to have induced Loehe to encourage the founding of a new synod that might mediate the differences between the Missourians and Grabau.

In the fall of 1853 a party of Loehe adherents left the Franconian communities in Michigan and migrated to Dubuque, Iowa. A portion of the group remained in Dubuque while the rest continued on to St. Sebald, 60 miles to the northwest. There, in 1854, the Iowa Synod was founded.[39] Loehe's influence remained strong throughout the history of the Iowa Synod, especially in its adoption and use of Loehe's *Agende* as the norm for the conduct of public worship. Layriz's influence in the Iowa Synod was exercised especially through the liturgical settings for pastor and congregation that he prepared for the second edition of Loehe's *Agende*.[40]

The situation was somewhat different with regard to

hymnody. At the second meeting of the Iowa Synod in 1855, at which time Grabau requested that the young synod take charge of the Buffalo Synod's congregations around Madison, Wisconsin; Detroit, Michigan; and Toledo, Ohio, it was resolved to introduce Grabau's hymnbook into the Iowa Synod on the condition that a new edition would take into consideration the particular needs of the Iowa Synod.[41] These conditions apparently were never fulfilled and the Iowa Synod began a period in which it became impossible to unify the synod around a single hymnbook. The hymnbooks which the various congregations chose to use—among them Grabau's hymnbook, Walther's St. Louis hymnbook, Raumer's hymnbook, and others from Bavaria[42]—reflected largely their earlier background or the associations that existed between particular pastors or congregations and other Lutheran groups in America.

In 1860 Prof. Fritschel traveled to Germany, at which time he requested a pastor Crome in Prussia to prepare a hymnbook for the Iowa Synod, but nothing came of this. By 1864 the synod resolved to make a selection of 150 hymns from the "Unverfaelschen Liedersegen," a collection of songs published in Berlin a few years earlier. While this was soon accomplished, it was readily acknowledged that it was merely an emergency measure.[43]

After the disruption of the General Synod in 1866, the Iowa Synod took an active part in the meetings that led to the formation of the General Council in 1867. While the Iowa Synod ultimately did not join the General Council because it regarded its attitude toward the "Four Points"[44] as unsatisfactory, two members of the Iowa Synod actively participated on the committee that ultimately produced the General Council's *Kirchenbuch* in 1877. These men were pastors G. M. Grossmann, president of the Iowa Synod from its founding until 1893, and Siegmund Fritschel.[45] The Iowa Synod resolved to introduce the *Kirchenbuch* into its congregations, and with its appearance in 1877 it was received into use in many of its congregations.

The "New Pennsylvania Hymnbook" of 1849

The Pennsylvania Ministerium had taken no part in the preparation of the *Evangelische Liedersammlung* of 1833, having left the General Synod in 1823 due, in part, to a fear of a too-strong central authority. By 1847, however, the Pennsylvania Ministerium had recognized the necessity of a new German hymnbook and issued a friendly invitation to the New York Ministerium to join with it in preparing such a book.[46]

The hymnal that resulted appeared in 1849 as the *Deutsches Gesangbuch fuer die Evangelisch-Lutherische Kirche in den Vereinigten Staaten.*[47] It was largely the work of Dr. C. R. Demme, pastor of St. Michael and Zion congregations in Philadelphia. Demme's *Deutsches Gesangbuch* contained 710 hymns and was commonly known as the "Wollenweber book" from the name of the publisher. This hymnbook drew over 300 of its hymns from a 1842 hymnbook of Wuerttemberg; the remaining hymns were drawn largely from Gerhardt, Rambach, Schmolke, and some from the period of rationalism.[48] Compared to the work of Quitman or the German hymnbook of the General Synod, Demme's work was a step in the right direction. However, it also inspired sharp criticism from the Missouri Synod in a series of four articles in *Der Lutheraner* in 1850.[49] In contrast to what the correspondent considered the "rein lutherische St. Louis Gesangbuch" (the "pure Lutheran St. Louis hymnal") he can only comment regarding the new Pennsylvania hymnbook:

But how dreadfully one is deceived in that, although a significant number of the old normative core-hymns may be found in this newly-published "German-Lutheran Hymnbook"—as one example, the old hymn of Gustavus Adolphus, "O little flock, fear not the foe," which is missing even in the St. Louis hymnal—nevertheless, many other principal hymns are not to be found but rather a hodgepodge of the same kind which one already found formerly in the

"Common Hymnbook."[50]

In a similar fashion the deleting of stanzas and similar editorial practices are also criticized.

> And how shamefully is Luther's hymn "Christ our Lord to Jordan came" distorted and mutilated. This powerful hymn of Luther had seven stanzas in the old hymnbook, but in the new "Pennsylvania" hymnal only three corrupted stanzas. And all stanzas of "All mankind fell in Adam's fall" have been so altered that one can hardly recognize the hymn. So greatly have the "preserving hands"—so named in the foreword to this hymnal—distorted and falsified this magnificent hymn which the Lutheran Church calls to our attention in the Book of Concord in the article on the "Freedom of the Will.*

> [*The article is in error; the reference occurs in the Formula of Concord in the article on "Original Sin."]

> I must confess that before I had seen the hymnal I myself in reality thought significantly more of it, although I do not deny that I was filled with strong suspicions against it, especially when I found out that S. S. Schmucker, the well-known falsifier of Lutheran teaching and the principal person responsible for the "new standards," had also been named a member of the hymnal committee.[51]

The criticisms throughout these four articles suggest that the Lutheran doctrine of the Lord's Supper had been altered, that many of the old *Kernlieder* have been left out, and that stanzas had been omitted. The conclusion to these articles characterized the serious concern for the hymnody of the church that marked the early days of The Lutheran Church—Missouri Synod.

> May the God of grace keep us in the pure evangelical truth, and may the church, as the bearer of the truth, serve to preserve the glorious treasure of her hymns uncorrupted until the end of days when the church militant will be translated to the eternal church triumphant.[52]

In part such criticisms were correct; Demme had made many changes in the old hymns. Observing that he did not regard these hymns "as having a canonical character, or as taking rank alongside of the Confessions of the church, or left behind by their authors as gifts which should not be touched," Demme made changes that frequently involved subtle alterations in doctrinal emphases. It was this practice that drew such criticism from the Missouri Synod. Demme's practice, however, represented the generally prevailing view.

On a more positive note, *The Evangelical Review*, marking the appearance of this new hymnbook, could say of these alterations, "Their changes we think are generally judicious, and some of them made with extraordinary skill."[53] But even the author of this review could not agree with the alterations made in Luther's "Lord Jesus Christ to Jordan came."[54]

In 1850 it was reported to the Pennsylvania Ministerium that a "Mr. Radde of New York has undertaken to print a piractical [sic] edition of our work, and append to it a Hymn Book compiled by himself."[55] This pirated edition was apparently *Das neue gemeinschaftliche Gesangbuch* published in 1850 in New York and which had incorporated Demme's *Deutsches Gesangbuch* as an appendix to the book.[56] In the light of this situation the Pennsylvania Ministerium resolved that

> . . . inasmuch as the Synod has been informed, that in some places the opinion has become prevalent that the Hymn Book published by Mr. Radde in 1850, may be used in connection with our own, it be hereby declared to those congregations that have introduced or may introduce our book, that such an opinion is unfounded.[57]

Apparently in an effort to avoid the consequences of such official reproach, the title *Das neue gemeinschaftliche Gesangbuch* was later changed to *Das neue lutherische Gesangbuch*,[58] a change that brought renewed pleas by the church bodies for increased attention to the contents of its hymnbooks.

A comparison of Demme's *Deutsches Gesangbuch* of 1849 with either Grabau's or Walther's *Kirchengesangbuch* of 1842 or 1847 respectively, is most interesting. Demme's hymnbook reflects a developing Lutheran consciousness that was still struggling toward a more firm confessional basis; Walther's and Grabau's books represent a confessionalism that had come to America firmly committed from the start to restore the hymnody of the Reformation. Demme's "new Pennsylvania hymnbook" continued in use in some places into the 20th century. It appeared in 1891 in a new and enlarged edition, adding 90 hymns to the original 710 hymns that remained exactly as in the original printing.[59]

The Efforts of the Ohio Synod

The early Lutherans who made their way into the Northwest Territory at the close of the 18th and beginning of the 19th centuries were served by pastors sent largely from the Pennsylvania Ministerium.[60] About the same time Paul Henkel began to make missionary journeys throughout Ohio. Yearly meetings of a "Special Conference" of the Lutheran ministers west of the Alleghenies were held from 1812 to 1818 when permission was obtained from the Pennsylvania Ministerium to organize a separate Ministerium. At one point this "Special Conference" resolved to publish a hymnbook and appointed a committee to make the selection of the hymns.[61] At first, with the formation in 1818 of the "General Conference of Ev. Lutheran preachers in the State of Ohio and Adjacent States," later reorganized in 1833 as the Joint Synod of Ohio, the congregations of this Lutheran body were forced to rely on whatever hymnbooks they might have at hand.

In 1843, at a special meeting of the Western District of the Joint Synod of Ohio, action was taken regarding a hymnbook.

Upon the request of the Miami Conference, a committee was

appointed, together with Dr. Demme in Philadelphia, to consider the matter of a new German hymnbook.

The involvement of this group in the preparation of such a hymnbook is uncertain, but in 1849 the Pennsylvania Ministerium issued its *Deutsches Gesangbuch* prepared under the direction of Dr. C. R. Demme. Demme's hymnbook of 1849 apparently served many congregations of the Joint Synod of Ohio, for in September 1850, the Eastern District of the Joint Synod of Ohio strongly recommended its use.[62] The time when the Joint Synod of Ohio was to produce its one and only German hymnbook was still 20 years away.

By 1864 the confessional revival in American Lutheranism was in full swing, and the reaction against the alteration and dilution of the original texts was gaining ground. That year the Joint Synod of Ohio, at the request of its Western District,[63] resolved to produce "A pure Lutheran hymnbook with unchanged and undiluted texts."[64] The committee named to produce this hymnbook consisted of G. Cronewett, W. F. Lehmann, M. Loy, E. Schmid, and F. A. Herzberger.[65] Admitting they did not always have the original texts of some of the hymns at hand, the committee, nevertheless, attempted, as best it could, to restore the original readings. A preliminary edition of the contemplated hymnbook appeared in 1867 for examination and, following a synodical resolution of 1868, several old and a few new hymns were added.

Two years earlier the Joint Synod of Ohio had appointed a committee to confer with the Missouri Synod to pave the way for friendly relations, and in a special meeting in Hamilton, Ohio, in June 1867, repeated the resolution with special reference to the cooperation of the Missouri Synod and the General Council in the publication of a new Lutheran hymnbook.[66] Although representatives of the Joint Synod of Ohio and the Missouri Synod reached accord in theological matters by March 1868, nothing came of the projected joint hymnbook with either the Missouri Synod or the General Council. That same year, the Joint Synod of

Ohio, finding the newly-formed General Council less orthodox than it anticipated, withdrew from the General Council.

Especially irritating to the Ohio Synod was the fact that the *Kirchengesangbuch* of the Missouri Synod had been introduced into many Ohio Synod congregations.[67] With its efforts to effect a joint hymnbook thwarted, the Joint Synod of Ohio proceeded alone. In 1879 it published its *Gesangbuch fuer Gemeinden des Evangelisch Lutherischen Bekenntnisses.*[68] It contained 532 hymns, several orders of service based on the Saxon and Pommeranian orders, and a selection of prayers.

The publication of this book marked a decided return to the use of a significant portion of that normative core of 16th-century Reformation hymnody, and a turning away from the deletion of stanzas and the looser editorial practices that characterized much of 19th-century American Lutheran hymnody. This book consciously sought to appropriate once again the hymnody of the Lutheran Reformation. The Ohio Synod *Gesangbuch* went through at least 22 editions and was used well into the beginning of the 20th century.

As far as the English language hymnody of the Ohio Synod is concerned, in its early years it used the General Synod's hymnbook of 1828, *Hymns, selected and original.*[69] The inadequacy of this book was readily apparent, especially in the light of the Ohio Synod's general confessional orientation. By 1843 the Western District of the Ohio Synod named a committee to produce an English hymnal. The result was *A Collection of Hymns and Prayers*[70] published in 1845. The chief sources for this collection, virtually the only ones at hand, were the General Synod's hymnbook and Quitman's New York collection. Predictably, the first English hymnbook of the Ohio Synod soon proved unsuitable, and before a decade had passed, plans were being formulated for a new and better book.[71] This new collection appeared about 1855, perhaps shortly before, as the *Collection of Hymns for Public and Private Worship*[72] containing 354 hymns and 7 doxologies. It included 50 translations from the German and was in Benson's view a "sincere and not ineffective effort to make a Lutheran hymnbook."[73] The committee that prepared the book acknowledged the sorry state of "our rather barren English hymnody"[74] and pointed to this fact as the reason for their inability to comply more fully with their instructions "to adapt the hymn-book to the ecclesiastical year."[75] In the light of a developing Lutheran confessionalism, the Ohio Synod's *Collection of Hymns for Public and Private Worship* was only a small step in the direction of recovering for the church the hymnody of the Reformation. But it was a step in the right direction.[76] This second Ohio Synod English hymnbook continued through four editions.

In June 1867, at a meeting of the Ohio Synod, the matter of a new edition of an English hymnbook was referred to the hymnbook committee.[77] The results of their work appeared 13 years later in 1880 with the publication of the *Evangelical Lutheran Hymnal*.[78] This collection represented a vigorous return to the hymnody of the Lutheran Reformation. Of the 468 hymns it contained, 181 or almost 40 percent were translations from the German, including many *Kernlieder*. In addition, the hymnbook contained 19 doxologies, together with Luther's Small Catechism, the Augsburg Confession, the Epistles and Gospels, the Passion history, and a collection of prayers. A music edition containing an additional 48 hymns was published in 1908.[79]

Although the early English hymnody of the Ohio Synod reflected the influences of the unionism and rationalism of those days, its contacts with the Missouri Synod in the "Free Conferences" of the 1850s and its membership in the Synodical Conference, organized in 1872, moved to strengthen and reinforce its inherent confessionalism. In its *Evangelical Lutheran Hymnal* of 1880 it went far beyond the General Council's *Church Book* of 1868 in appropriating for English-speaking Lutherans the historic heritage of Reformation hymnody. It is to the story of the General Council's *Church Book* that we now turn.

The General Council's *Church Book* of 1868

In 1862 the Ministerium of Pennsylvania actively entered the field of English Lutheran hymnody. That year Dr. Wm. J. Mann, president of the Ministerium, called for "an improved English Hymn Book . . . more fully in harmony with the spirit of our Church"[80] and appointed as a committee Revs. C. W. Schaeffer, G. F. Krotel, B. M. Schmucker, A. T. Geissenhaimer, C. F. Welden, F. W. Conrad, and J. Kohler to begin work.[81] Also invited to associate himself with the committee was the Rev. Frederick Mayer Bird of the New York Ministerium who was to exert a profound influence on the course of American Lutheran hymnody.

After reviewing all the English hymnbooks it could find, the committee judged all of them unsatisfactory and resolved that a new hymnbook should be prepared containing an "ample selection of hymns, with special reference to the doctrines and usages of our Church."[82] The result of the committee's work, guided principally by B. M. Schmucker and Bird,[83] was a provisional edition[84] printed in 1865 for examination and review before it would appear in permanent form. A notice of publication indicates that the collection contained 628 hymns and 18 doxologies.[85]

Concerning this provisional hymnbook, the English Minutes of the Pennsylvania Ministerium of 1865 contain the following report.

> It seems hardly necessary to say that it has been the earnest and constant aim of the workers in this matter that the English Hymn Book should meet the wants of the Church and not be unworthy of the character and principles of this Synod. They have endeavored to supply the deficiencies of English hymnody by as large an infusion of German and Latin (and Greek) matter as was possible, and about one-fourth the contents of the book consists of translations from these and other foreign sources.[86]

A review of this provisional book provides more

information of interest.

> Whilst admitting "no hymn in conflict with the doctrine, spirit and usages of the Lutheran Church," they determined to make a hymnal, not narrow or bigoted, but broad, liberal, and Catholic.

> About two hundred and fourteen of these hymns are found in the General Synod's Hymn Book, comprising the mass of those commonly used. More than one hundred hymns are by the Wesleys, about eighty by Dr. Watts, and a considerable number by Cowper, Steele, Toplady, Doddrige, Mason, and other authors less known. One hundred hymns are of German origin, and forty-seven of Greek and Latin.[87]

In spite of the "infusion of German, Latin [and Greek] matter," the predominant bias in favor of English hymnody is clearly evident.

> In the old Hymn Book, of one thousand hymns, about fifty-three only are by the Wesleys: in this new Hymn Book we have more than one hundred, or about one-sixth of the whole number. . . . Charles Wesley's hymns, taken as a whole, are the best in the English language and, excepting some ideosyncracies, accord more with the doctrine and spirit of our Church than any other. Whilst we admire many of the smooth and beautiful lyrics of Watts, we are more in sympathy with the natural, soulful sweetness and glowing thought of the Hymn Poet of Methodism, than with the classic correctness and beauty of the bard of Calvinism.[88]

The translations from the German presented a special problem. Commenting on the General Synod's earlier hymnbook, *Hymns, selected and original* of 1828, which had been in use for over a quarter century, Wedell remarked:

> Its only marked feature was an attempt to introduce into our Churches a mass of unpoetical trash, called, by courtesy, translations from the German, which resembled the originals as much as the miserable daubs of some awkward artist

resemble the paintings of the great masters, and from which they recopied.[89]

The introduction of the German translations in the General Synod's hymnbook was not only viewed as a failure, but it "created a prejudice against all efforts in that direction"[90] as well. In approaching the matter of the German translations in Schmucker and Bird's hymnbook, the reviewer in the *Evangelical Review* admittedly expected little.

> They [the German translations] compare very favorably with their English associates. We were unprepared for this result. Taking our pencil to note their character, we expected to place at least the half of them, under the head of "condemned articles," upon examination, however, we found but few to which we would object.[91]

But the pervasiveness of the general bias against such translations was evident. In Wedell's view, "the number is [still] too great."[92]

But ecclesiastical considerations were to intervene and prevent the final publication of this provisional hymnbook in the way originally envisioned by the Pennsylvania Ministerium. A year prior to the issuing of this provisional collection, the Pennsylvania Ministerium had withdrawn from the General Synod because of the admission of the more liberal Franckean Synod to the General Synod. Under the leadership of Charles Porterfield Krauth, who together with J. A. Seiss had been added to the hymnbook committee, the Pennsylvania Ministerium took a leading part in the formation of the General Council in 1867.

With the revision of its provisional hymnbook nearing completion in 1866, the Pennsylvania Ministerium postponed action regarding the publication of this collection in permanent form, and decided to present to the Reading convention—a preliminary meeting prior to the formal organization of the General Council—its desire for uniformity in public worship.[93] The Reading convention, in

December 1866, appointed a committee to cooperate with the Pennsylvania Ministerium regarding a hymnbook and a common liturgy.[94]

The General Council was formally established in 1867. With the Pennsylvania Ministerium as one of its leaders, the General Council, meeting in Fort Wayne, Indiana, accepted the proposal of the joint committee and resolved

> That the General Council heartily concur in the propriety and necessity of the publication of a work of the kind proposed, and hereby accept and authorize the publication of the English Church Book prepared by the Ministerium of Pennsylvania.
>
> [Also] That the Collection of Hymns made by the Ministerium of Pennsylvania, as finally reviewed by them, be inserted.[95]

This collection appeared in 1868 as the *Church Book For the Use of Evangelical Lutheran Congregations*,[96] published in Philadelphia by authority of the General Council, the copyright, however, remaining with the Pennsylvania Ministerium, which had been almost exclusively responsible for the selection of hymns in the collection.

In 1869 the committee was instructed "to select music for the English Church Book"[97] and the results appeared in 1872 as the *Church Book With Music arranged for the use of congregations*. The editor was Harriet Reynolds Krauth, the only woman who has ever served as music editor of an American Lutheran hymnal.[98] A somewhat revised edition was published in 1891, the Pennsylvania Ministerium having transferred its property rights to the book to the General Council. At a meeting of the General Council in 1891 the committee reported on the completion of this revised edition, commenting that the *Church Book* was "the most complete publication of the kind ever issued by the Lutheran Church, in this or other countries."[99]

In appraising this work, Reed has suggested that the *Church Book* "was unquestionably the best liturgy and hymnal which the Lutheran Church in America has yet produced."[100] Benson was equally high in his praise.

There was at the time no American hymnal so fully representative of the development of Hymnody, so discriminating in selection, so scholarly in treatment.

In Miss Krauth's musical setting the German choral is fittingly preeminent, supplemented by the English tunes most in accord with its spirit; and the concessions to popular demand are comparatively slight. English speaking Lutheranism had at last expressed itself in a hymnal worthy of its own traditions, and on a plane where no other American denomination could hope to meet it.[101]

Benson's remark that no other hymnal in America was "so fully representative of the development of Hymnody" is certainly true. Yet the importance of this hymnbook as representative of a specifically Lutheran hymnody, particularly Lutheran hymnody of the Reformation's early formative years, is somewhat mitigated by the fact that less than one-sixth of the total contents could in any way be described as specifically Lutheran.

This is thoroughly understandable in view of the temper of the times and the personal predilections of the compilers, particularly Frederick Bird. The entire history of English-language Lutheran hymnody in America had shown an aversion to English translations of its German heritage, almost from the very first. Moreover, at this time a new era in the history of English hymnody was opening up as a result of the Oxford Movement and the work of such men as John Mason Neale, Edward Caswall, and others who were recovering the riches of Greek and Latin hymnody in English translations. *Hymns Ancient and Modern*[102], a landmark collection in English hymnody, had been published in England in 1861. All this work was available to the committee and immeasurably enriched their work, a fact evident from the heavy use made of these resources.[103] The work of Catherine Winkworth, Richard Massie, and others who were exploring the riches of German hymnody and providing noteworthy English translations were also beginning to be used. Bird made a particular point of commending this material. Yet he recognized that the use of such translations was in opposition to the prevailing mood of the day in America.

> We must get rid of a notion which many people, knowing precisely nothing about the matter, have deeply imbibed, and are disposed strenuously to insist upon: that translated hymns, whether German, Latin, or what, can be of no use. . . .[104]

In the very year the *Church Book* was first published, Bird departed the Lutheran Church and entered the ministry of the Episcopal Church.[105] All these factors seem to suggest strongly that, while giving full recognition to Bird's hymnological eminence and contribution, he apparently felt no great personal responsibility for the development of a specifically Lutheran hymnody for the Lutheran church in America. It is interesting to note in this context that while Benson can speak of the General Council's *Church Book* as the foremost hymnbook of the time, and that no other was so "fully representative of the development of Hymnody," he could, at the same time, speak of the *Evangelical Lutheran Hymn-Book* of 1889, published by the General English Conference of Missouri and Other States, as unquestionably "the most distinctively Lutheran of all the hymn books."[106] It is precisely in the appropriation—or the lack of appropriation—of that normative core of Reformation hymnody that Benson's distinction between a hymnbook "fully representative of the development of Hymnody" and one "distinctively Lutheran" must be seen.

The General Council's *Kirchenbuch* of 1877

The work of the General Council not only concerned itself with an English hymnbook. At its first regular convention in 1867 in Fort Wayne, Indiana, the General Council also made preparation for the publication of a German hymnbook that would also reflect the growing concern for a more confessional hymnody.[107] A committee consisting of Dr. A.

147

Spaeth, B. M. Schmucker, C. F. Moldenke, and S. Fritschel was appointed to prepare the hymnbook.[108] Among the guidelines which the committee was to use in the selection of hymns were the following:

1. That in the Hymn Book to be published by the General Council, all those hymns should be first collected which we find contained in the best Lutheran Hymn Books.
2. That the hymns to be received should be adopted in their original form, but that this should not be interpreted as allowing of no exception.
3. That only such changes should be made as are already embodied in good Lutheran Hymn Books.
4. That hymns, in which considerable changes are necessary, should not be embodied in the Hymn Book.
5. That a sub-committee should be appointed, on the basis of the canon given above, and making use of the books now under course of preparation by the Synods of Ohio and Wisconsin, should prepare a provisional Hymn Book.[109]

The emphasis on the original forms of the hymn texts was in rather direct contrast to the procedure employed in Demme's *Deutsches Gesangbuch* of 1849 and was a good omen for Lutheran hymnody in America.

By 1870 the committee reported the publication of a Provisional German Hymn Book which was referred to the district synods for careful examination.[110] Seven years later, in 1877, the new General Council's German hymnal appeared as the *Kirchenbuch fuer Evangelisch-Lutherische Gemeinden*, containing 595 hymns, most of them from the 16th and 17th centuries in their original textual and melodic form. The *Kirchenbuch* was published in a large and small edition, and it was reported that music for the book was in the course of publication.[111]

Two years later, in 1879, the *Choralbuch mit Liturgie und Chorgesaengen zum Kirchenbuch der Allgemeinen Kirchenversammlung*,[112] "prepared by John Endlich at the request and with the approbation of the committee, furnishing the full musical material for the *Kirchenbuch*, was reported in the hands of the printer"[113] and appeared that same year. Regarding Endlich's *Choralbuch*, the committee remarked:

> It has been most carefully prepared from the best sources of pure church music and deserved to be most heartily recommended to all the congregations using the Church Book. It is hardly possible to do full justice to the German Church Book, and to make its rich treasures fully understood and enjoyed by our churches without this book which furnished the complete musical material for both liturgy and the hymns of our Church Book, adding besides a number of the finest and purest anthems [*Chorgesaenge*] of the eighteenth century.[114]

Endlich's concern is well stated in the Preface to the *Choralbuch*.

> This laborious and expensive task was undertaken without any thought of remuneration or honor, but out of an inner desire to restore to the church also the musical settings which have been lacking in the past, as the Church-Book has already accomplished in hymn and word. In Germany much laudable work has been done in this respect compared with the little work done here in America. Without the motivation of the Church-book, we would have to wait even longer to recapture the stately old chorales and liturgical settings.[115]

The chief source for the liturgical settings in the *Choralbuch* was the scholarly research of Ludwig Schoeberlein; the sources for the chorale settings were the works of Tucher, Layriz, Zahn, and others. Endlich could speak of the "herrliche rhythmische Choral" and encourage its use in both German and English services.[116]

At the time of the introduction of the *Kirchenbuch*, the so-called "common hymnbooks" were still in rather wide use and presented a continuing problem. In 1877, with the introduction of the *Kirchenbuch*, the New York Ministerium took specific action to bring the use of "common hymnbooks" to an end, the president of the Ministerium noting that these books were un-Lutheran and urged all their congregations to introduce the *Kirchenbuch* instead.[117]

By 1888 Nicum could report that the *Kirchenbuch* was in use in the great majority of General Council congregations that employed the German language.[118]

The General Council's *Kirchenbuch* was the last major collection of German Lutheran hymnody in America. After its appearance in 1877, no American Lutheran church body produced a significantly new addition to the corpus of German language hymnody. The reason was readily apparent. By the close of the 19th century the transition to a completely English language hymnody among American Lutherans was in full swing. While various Lutheran groups continued to make German hymnbooks available for those congregations which still clung to that language, it was clear that the generation growing up at the beginning of the 20th century was the last for which German hymnody would continue to be a live option. It only remained for the following generation to make the transition complete.

The Transition to English in the Missouri Synod and the *Evangelical Lutheran Hymn-Book* of 1912

The actual transition to an English-language hymnody in the Missouri Synod began in the last quarter of the 19th century. While the greater part of this church's missionary endeavor was directed to the constant stream of German immigrants flocking to America in the last decades of the century, the need for English-language services and for an English-language hymnody became increasingly apparent. As the hymnody of this immigrant body made the transition, its concern for both a confessional hymnody and the rhythmic chorale was vigorously maintained.

Walther himself encouraged the use of a small collection of English hymns—*Hymnbook for the use of Evangelical Lutheran Schools and Congregations*[119]—published by the Norwegians in 1879 in Decorah, Iowa. The favorable impression which this volume made on Walther,[120] together with the increasing necessity for an English hymnody, gave encouragement to the production of three small English-language hymnbooks, all of quite modest scope, with the specific objective of serving as a resource for special congregational services requiring hymns in English, as well as a resource for the introduction of English services in congregations that had been exclusively German.

The first of these books was *Lutheran Hymns, For the Use of English Lutheran Missions*[121] published in 1882. It was a slender collection of 18 of the most familiar German hymns with melodies in translations by Martin Guenther and C. Janzow. In 1886 a somewhat similar collection appeared as *Hymns of the Evangelical Lutheran Church. For the Use of English Lutheran Missions,*[122] a collection of 33 hymns with melodies collected and edited by Prof. August Crull. In 1905 Prof. F. Bente of Concordia Seminary, St. Louis, prepared a hymnal of 199 hymns without music entitled *Hymns for Evangelical Lutheran Missions.*[123]

These three modest hymnbooks were somewhat tentative experiments in the period of transition to an English-language hymnody in the Missouri Synod. The major effort was an English hymnbook prepared in the late 1880s by August Crull of Fort Wayne. It was presented by Crull to the English Lutheran Conference of Missouri and accepted by them at their meeting in St. Louis in 1888.[124] This hymnbook, published in Baltimore in 1889 by the Lutheran Publication Board for the Conference, was the *Evangelical Lutheran Hymn Book.*[125] The book contained 400 hymns, the 3 ecumenical creeds, the Augsburg Confession, and an order for morning and evening services. A new edition appeared in 1892 which added 50 hymns and the Common Service, Matins, and Vespers. This new edition, which contained only texts, was subsequently published in Pittsburgh and Chicago. This collection was the immediate forerunner of the book that was to become the first official English-language hymnbook of the Missouri Synod.

Crull's work on the *Evangelical Lutheran Hymn Book* did not concern itself with the music for the hymnal. By 1891, however, the English Lutheran Synod of Missouri, Ohio and

Other States had appointed a committee to prepare a music edition of the *Evangelical Lutheran Hymn Book.* [126] This work was not completed until 1911 when the English Synod of the Evangelical Lutheran Synod of Missouri, Ohio and Other States became the English District of the Evangelical Lutheran Synod of Missouri, Ohio and Other States. The music edition, which was now ready for publication, was presented to the new parent body, appearing in 1912 as the *Evangelical Lutheran Hymn-Book with Tunes,*[127] the first official English hymnbook of the Missouri Synod. Music editor, together with Hermann Polack (1862–1930), was Ludwig Herman Ilse (1845-1931).[128] He served with Hermann Polack as a special committee on the music for the hymnbook. [129] The collection included 567 hymns, a number of chants, doxologies, and a liturgical section that included the Common Service. This book was a significant milestone in recovering the Lutheran heritage of the 16th century in the English language. It was to serve the Missouri Synod until a later revision, involving in its preparation the other members of the Synodical Conference, appeared in 1941.

8

Movements Toward Consensus and Consolidation

Lutherans in America had always tended to group together with others of similar beliefs or with those with whom they shared a common vision for the church in the New World. The General Synod, organized in 1820 as a federation of Lutheran synods, was an early effort in that direction. The General Council, organized in 1867 as a more conservative grouping of synods who found the General Synod too lax, was a later example. With the movement of the Lutheran Church westward along the expanding frontier and the consequent increase in the number of Lutheran synods, fueled by the rapidly increasing numbers of Lutheran immigrants pouring into America in the 19th century, new groupings of Lutherans were inevitable.

Certainly many factors contributed toward an increasing interest in consensus and consolidation. For many it was a step toward more effectively and efficiently addressing those whom the church wanted to reach with the message of the Gospel. For others the unwieldy circumstances and the many difficulties presented by a proliferation of a large number of smaller synods was increasingly apparent. For still others the perpetuation of the culture and language of their parents' homeland—often the initial reason for the establishment of separate synods—was no longer felt to be either necessary or desirable. For many the gradual breaking down of the spirit of separatism as

Lutherans gradually became more attuned to the American situation together with the positive experiences of many Lutherans who had engaged in a variety of united efforts with other Lutherans, helped to create a climate in which united efforts seemed to make sense from many perspectives.

In many instances such united efforts were small in scope and local in their impact. In other cases they played themselves out on a larger scale. Perhaps the most dramatic of these united efforts as they related to worship was the experience of a significant portion of Lutherans in the development of the Common Service of 1888. The development of a Common Service for worship by the General Council, the General Synod, and the United Synod of the South in the years following the production of the *Church Book* of the General Council had far-reaching implications for all Lutherans as they made their way into the 20th century. It was quickly adopted by many Lutherans who had not taken part in its production, and the development and use of the Common Service was to remain a vital influence in American Lutheranism throughout most of the 20th century. It helped, as well, to establish a climate in which future efforts toward consolidation and consensus became more likely and more possible.

The *Lutheran Hymnary* of 1913

The first Lutheran hymnal to appear in the 20th century as a result of the movement toward consolidation and consensus was produced by three Norwegian churches: the United Norwegian Lutheran Church,[1] the Norwegian Lutheran Church,[2] and the Hauge Lutheran Synod.[3] The hymnbook was the result of the work of a committee of 12 members, four from each of the three church bodies. The committee was headed by John Dahle[4] with F. Melius Christiansen[5] serving as music editor. The factors that suggested the formation of a joint committee were spelled out in the Preface to the collection that ultimately appeared.

> The considerations which prompted the creation of the joint committee were, chiefly, the common need of an adequate and satisfactory English hymn book; the fact of a common faith and confession as well as a common inheritance of Lutheran hymnody; the probability of getting a better hymn book through united effort; and finally, the desirability of a common hymnary, especially in the event of a union of the Church bodies concerned.[6]

In fact, since 1905 these three synods had been working together toward the possibility of merger.[7] The committee had available to them the *Christian Hymns for Church, School and Home*[8] of the Norwegian Synod, and the *Church and Sunday School Hymnal*[9] of the United Norwegian Lutheran Church, both published in 1898. The new collection appeared in 1913 as *The Lutheran Hymnary*,[10] containing 618 hymns and 14 doxologies. Also included were two morning and two evening services, some litanies, the introits and collects for the church year, and selected psalms.

The hymnal set about "to embody in The Lutheran Hymnary the best translations of German and Norwegian Lutheran hymns."[11] While *The Lutheran Hymnary* contained nothing of the Swedish heritage of Christian song, it provided a rich treasury of Norwegian, Danish, and German Lutheran hymnody.

> The Norwegian Lutheran Church of America has inherited a rich treasury of hymns and chorals from the Mother Church; and while the Norwegian-American Church would secure this treasure and transmit it to her children, it is also hoped that the hymns of Kingo, Grundtvig, Brorson, Landstad, Brun and others, rendered into English, may prove attractive to the English bodies of the Church of the Reformation, and eventually find a place in their hearts and hymnals.[12]

The hymnbook included some 262 translations from the

Norwegian, together with 118 translations from German sources.

The Lutheran Hymnary consciously returned to a greater use of the chorale and represented a solid advance in reclaiming much of the historic hymnody of the Lutheran Church for English-speaking Lutherans. Speaking of the importance of the chorale, the editors could remark that "these chorals have survived the test of time and have proven their vitality and intrinsic value by long and constant use in the homes and sanctuaries of God's people."[13] Two other features of *The Hymnary* should be mentioned: the use of the rhythmic chorale and the arrangement of the hymns according to the church year. The Preface notes that

> Twenty German chorales are arranged in rhythmical meter; twenty have a melodic or contrapuntal setting. These special features the committee hopes will serve a purpose in discovering the wishes of the Church regarding the rhythmical form and the melodic arrangement of Lutheran chorals.[14]

Regarding the arrangement of the hymnal, it was hoped that

> the arrangement of the hymns according to the Sunday texts of the church year, a feature familiar from our Norwegian hymn books, will prove a valuable aid in selecting appropriate hymns for the services, and, better than a mere topical index, serve to promote a general use of the hymns found in the hymnal.[15]

In its return to the hymnody of the 16th-century Reformation, it was by far the best of the English hymnbooks produced by the various Scandinavian groups. In its return to the use of that normative core of Reformation hymnody, it was exceeded only by the Ohio Synod's *Evangelical Lutheran Hymnal* of 1880 and by the *Evangelical Lutheran Hymnbook* of the Missouri Synod, published a year earlier than *The Lutheran Hymnary*.

Three years following the publication of *The Lutheran Hymnary*, there appeared an unofficial book, *Concordia*,[16] published in 1916 in both English and Norwegian, and containing about 250 hymns, many of which were set to Scandinavian folk songs.[17] An enlarged edition containing 434 hymns appeared in 1932. Intended for youth and the needs of Sunday Schools, the collection became popular through its use of Scandinavian folk melodies and "in some circles of less liturgical tendencies in the church it succeeded in displacing *The Lutheran Hymnary*."[18]

In 1917, the 400th anniversary of the Lutheran Reformation, the three church bodies cooperating in *The Lutheran Hymnary*—the United Norwegian Lutheran Church, the Norwegian Lutheran Synod, and the Hauge Lutheran Synod—merged to form The Norwegian Lutheran Church of America, later known as the Evangelical Lutheran Church. *The Lutheran Hymnary* became the official book of that church body.

The *Common Service Book and Hymnal* of 1917

In the years following the appearance of the *Church Book* of the General Council, three Lutheran church bodies addressed themselves to the preparation of a "Common Service" that would hopefully serve to unite the Lutheran bodies of America in a common rite. This significant liturgical development came to fruition in 1888 when the General Synod, the General Council, and the United Synod of the South agreed on a basic text.[19] The emergence of the Common Service in 1888 provided the impetus for further united efforts by these three groups in the area of hymnody. By action of these three bodies, the joint committee which had prepared the Common Service was continued and, among other efforts, directed its attention to the preparation of a common hymnbook.

While the development of the Common Service was a signal achievement in the recovery of a distinctly Lutheran liturgical consciousness, the hymnbooks of the three groups involved in the preparation of the Common Service left much to be desired. The hymns of the General Synod's *Book of Worship* of 1880 were described by Luther Reed as "largely subjective and frequently Calvinistic in character. The only recognition accorded the church year was the inclusion of twenty hymns for church festivals."[20] In similar fashion, the *Book of Worship*[21] of the United Synod of the South contained hymns in which "subjective and Calvinistic elements preponderated in the hymnal."[22] In contrast, the *Church Book* of the General Council was, in Reed's view, "the best which the church had produced up to that time."[23] The situation seemed ripe because the appearance of the Common Service based on "the common consent of the pure Lutheran liturgies of the Sixteenth Century" was a good omen for the development of a common hymnbook. If a common hymnbook sought to reclaim for American Lutheranism the Reformation hymnody of that same period, it could be a significant milestone in the further development of a confessional Lutheran hymnody in America. In October 1897 the General Council resolved

> that the Church Book Committee be appointed to confer and cooperate with committees from any other Lutheran Bodies in the preparation of a Common Book of Worship, including, besides the Common Order of Service, Orders for Ministerial Acts, and a Book of Hymns in the English Language.[24]

By 1901 it was reported to the General Council that

> ... a Proof Copy of a Common Hymnal has been printed. About 450 hymns have been passed upon by the Joint Committee, and more than 300 of those have been approved for insertion in the new book.[25]

Two years later, in 1903, the Joint Committee, in an official statement to the general church bodies cooperating in this project, reported that the manuscript of the hymnbook had been completed.

> The manuscript of the Hymn Book . . . has been
> completed, and a synopsis and index of it are herewith
> submitted, with a statement of the principles which
> have governed its preparation and of the sources from
> which it has been derived. Your committee does not ask
> for your final approval of the Hymn Book, but it has
> submitted it at this time because the committee of the
> United Synod has urgently asked permission to print it
> for the use of the churches of that body.[26]

The General Synod had already consented to the
request of the United Synod of the South, and the Church
Book Committee of the General Council recommended that
the United Synod be given permission to publish the
manuscript hymnbook for its member churches, a
recommendation subsequently adopted by the General
Council. The United Synod of the South proceeded with the
publication of the hymnbook which had been completed by
the joint committee, and in 1907 the Church Book
Committee reported that the hymnbook had been published.

> The Hymnal has been published by the United Synod
> of the South, bound with the Common Service
> (Standard Edition), and has already gone through
> three editions.[27]

That the distribution of this hymnbook was not restricted to
the member churches of the United Synod of the South was
evident from the note that "it may be procured by the
members of this body [General Council] from our Board of
Publication at the special price of fifty cents a copy,
postpaid."[28] This hymnbook had not, however, been adopted
by either the General Council or the General Synod who
looked to still further revision of the hymnbook as
distributed by the United Synod of the South.

In 1909 the General Council meeting in Minneapolis
invited the cooperation of the General Synod and the United

Synod of the South in a final revision of the proposed common hymnbook.[29]

> A Sub-committee, consisting of Dr. Jacobs, Dr. Ohl, Mr. Steimle, and Mr. Reed,[30] then entered upon a most thorough examination of the arrangement and contents of the Common Hymnal, largely upon the basis of exhaustive studies by Dr. Jacobs in the history, contents and textual readings of standard hymns, and upon a principle of arrangement suggested by Dr. Schmauk. This included not only the entire field of English Hymnody, but translations from the hymns of the Early Church, the Latin, German, Swedish, Danish and Icelandic.[31]

The final report of the subcommittee on texts was examined by the Joint Committee in November 1911 and a printed proof copy came from the press in July 1912.[32] While the Joint Committee continued to make alterations in the selection and arrangement of the hymns, the essential character of what was to be the *Common Service Book and Hymnal* of 1917 was basically determined with this proof copy, if, indeed, its basic course had not already been largely determined by the time of the official statement of the Joint Committee in 1903. A brief summary of the origins of the hymns in the 1912 proof copy compared with the final result published in 1917 illustrates this clearly. Excluding examples of specific hymns, the balance of hymns of English, German, Greek, Latin, etc. origin in the final version did not change from the work accomplished by 1912.

Comparison of the Number of Hymns in the Proof Copy
(1912) with the Common Service Book and Hymnal
(1917)

	English	German	Latin	Greek	Other	Total
1912	425	126	55	11	12	629
	(67%)	(20%)	(8%)	(2%)	(2%)	

1917	397	118	45	9	9	578
	(68%)	(20%)	(7%)	(1.5%)	(1.5%)	

In 1917, the 400th anniversary of the Lutheran Reformation, the *Common Service Book and Hymnal*[33] appeared, the result of the joint effort of the General Synod, the General Council, and the United Synod of the South. The hymnbook contained 578 hymns with an appendix containing 19 alternate tunes. Rev. Jeremiah Ohl[34] served as chairman of the music sub-committee. The following year these three church bodies merged to form the United Lutheran Church in America.

The basic strength of the *Common Service Book and Hymnal* was to be found in the achievements of its liturgical formulations and in the fact that, for the first time, a significantly large group of American Lutherans were united about a common body of hymnody in their official book of worship. The weakness of the book was rooted in the attitude of its compilers toward the matter of translations and in the resulting failure to reclaim, to any significant degree, the historic, confessional hymnody of the 16th-century Lutheran Reformation to which its liturgy paid homage. These factors, crucial to the development of a truly confessional Lutheran hymnbook, prevented the *Common Service Book and Hymnal* from extending its excellence beyond that of its liturgical forms and into the content of its hymnody.

The exhaustive studies of the Joint Committee included

> translations from the hymns of the Early Church, the Latin, German, Swedish, Danish and Icelandic. Every number in the files of The Workman and of The Lutheran since 1866 was searched for . . . acceptable translations by American Lutherans.[35]

The search apparently was in vain. The standard of "literary merit,"[36] one of the overriding concerns of the committee in the assembling of this hymnbook, apparently precluded the

Joint Committee's use of the translations that were available.

> No effort or expense was spared in gathering all books
> in which English translations of the treasures of
> Lutheran hymnody in other languages, are found. . . .
> *The great bulk of this vast material was absolutely
> unusable.* The difference in the structure of the
> languages, stands in the way of idiomatic translations.
> [Emphasis mine][37]

Not only was this attitude toward the translations readily
available evident in the almost complete lack of that
normative core of Reformation hymnody in the *Common
Service Book and Hymnal,* but it prevented, as well, the great
heritage of Scandinavian Lutheran hymnody from making
any contribution toward this hymnbook.[38]

> The committee was eager to have the Lutheran
> Hymnody of other languages than German represented
> by translations. But, on examination, many of the best
> hymns in Scandinavian collections, proved to be little
> more than translations or paraphrases of German
> hymns, translations of which had already been
> included. Selections of other hymns were repeatedly
> made by a sub-committee, which failed to satisfy the
> committee as a whole, because the translation fell
> beneath the required standard.[39]

The lack of the Scandinavian heritage of Lutheran hymnody
in the *Common Service Book and Hymnal* was keenly felt
and sharply expressed, as the following typical comment
clearly indicates.

> The Common Service Book and Hymnal is no doubt an
> excellent production. . . . Nevertheless, the fact that
> the committee rigorously guarded the hymnal against
> the introduction of renditions of Norwegian, Swedish or
> Danish hymns as found in The Lutheran Hymnary,
> persistently ignoring these translations, is a loss to the
> hymnal and to be regretted. . . . The omission, whether

by design or inadvertence, is a disappointment to the Scandinavian-American Lutherans. . . . A hymnbook which purports to serve the Church at large may not confine itself to the choice of the literary and musical productions of one section of the Church.[40]

It remains an enigma that in a book which determined its liturgical formulations on the basis of the "common consent of the pure Lutheran Liturgies of the Sixteenth Century," the contents of the hymnbook should avoid so radically the Lutheran heritage of hymnody of that same century for a hymnody in which literary merit, extent of usage, and agreement with the spirit and faith of the Lutheran Church—*in that order*—should determine congregational song. The reasons behind this enigma can be found in the developing histories of the church bodies that joined together in its production and in the personal proclivities of its compilers. Neither the General Synod, the United Synod of the South, nor the General Council had utilized to any significant degree in their earlier English hymnody that normative core of Lutheran hymnody from the 16th-century Lutheran Reformation. In addition, the chief concern and major attention of the Joint Committee seems to have been directed, first of all, to the further refinement of the Common Service together with its allied orders, an area of work in which the committee did exceptionally excellent work. The final result was a Common Service that was a truly remarkable production coupled with a hymnbook still quite removed from a distinctly confessional Lutheran collection.

The *American Lutheran Hymnal* of 1930

It was the hope of the framers of the *Common Service Book and Hymnal* that it might be accepted by most of the Lutheran bodies in America. However, while most Lutheran

163

church bodies rather quickly adopted the Common Service, printing it in their hymnbooks alongside their own traditional orders, they continued to use their own collections of hymns. Thus in 1918 the *Wartburg Hymnal for Church, School, and Home*[41] had been published for use in the Iowa Synod as a temporary measure until such a time as a more adequate collection could be prepared. In this context and at the invitation of the Iowa Synod, representatives of eight Lutheran church bodies met in Chicago, Illinois, on May 3, 1921, to explore the possibility of creating an inter-synodical hymnbook that would meet with greater acceptance than had the *Common Service Book and Hymnal*.

Chairman of the intersynodical committee was Emmanuel Poppen, prominent pastor in the Ohio Synod and, later, second president of the American Lutheran Church. The committee worked for nine years, the results of their work appearing in 1930 as the *American Lutheran Hymnal*[42], a collection of 651 hymns. The same year the hymnbook appeared, three of the member church bodies that had worked on the hymnbook—the Iowa Synod, the Ohio Synod, and the Buffalo Synod—merged to form the American Lutheran Church.[43] Of those who had worked on the preparation of this collection, only the American Lutheran Church officially adopted the hymnbook. The time was not yet ripe for a hymnbook that would be used by the majority of Lutherans in America.

Textually, the *American Lutheran Hymnal* attempted to include hymns from the heritage of the ancient church, from the German and Scandinavian churches, as well as from the treasury of English hymns.

> Both those who prefer the ancient hymns and the texts of German and Scandinavian chorales, which have come to us in translations, as well as those who have greater liking for hymns originally written in the English language, will find that ample provision has been made to meet their need or preference.[44]

Musically, "as a rule, the original rhythmical form of the German chorales has been used in the Music Edition of the Hymnal."[45] This hymnal marked a significant advance over the hymnals published by the Swedish immigrants in 1925 and the Danish immigrants in 1927, particularly in the reintroduction of many of the hymns of the Lutheran Reformation. The Ohio, Iowa, and Buffalo Synods had come to this joint project with strong confessional convictions that were clearly evident in the hymnody it chose.[46]

By 1945, fifteen years after the appearance of the *American Lutheran Hymnal,* the American Lutheran Church had joined with the Evangelical Lutheran Church, the United Lutheran Church, and the Augustana Lutheran Church in the preparation of what would be the *Service Book and Hymnal* of 1958.

The Synodical Conference
and *The Lutheran Hymnal* of 1941

The Evangelical Lutheran Synodical Conference of North America was organized in 1872 by six conservative Lutheran synods who felt that a new general Lutheran body, organized strictly along confessional lines and free from unionistic practices, was necessary for the spread of true Lutheran unity. The organization was, in part, a natural consequence of the "free conferences" of the 1850s and, more immediately, of the failure of the General Council in the years immediately following its organization in 1867, to display to the satisfaction of more conservative Lutheran groups a more consistent Lutheran position, especially on the so-called Four Points.[47]

The six synods that organized the Synodical Conference were the synods of Ohio, Missouri, Wisconsin, Illinois, Minnesota, and the Norwegian Synod. While the election controversy of the 1880s brought about the withdrawal of the Ohio and Norwegian Synods, several other bodies joined in the ensuing years.[48] Since the Synodical Conference was a federation, not a merger, of synods, the constituent bodies were free to continue to use the hymnals in their possession. The concern for a confessional hymnody, however, was taken seriously and the subject of Lutheran hymnody was not absent from its deliberations.

Wilhelm Sihler, author of a set of theses concerning church fellowship presented at the second meeting of the Synodical Conference in 1873, pointed to the importance of pure church books.

> Furthermore, it is a denial of the Confessions when a Lutheran body does not maintain that only orthodox agendas, hymnals, catechisms, religious textbooks, and devotional material should be used, or yet when proper diligence is not exerted to remove unorthodox books of this kind which are presently being used and to introduce orthodox ones.[49]

The discussion of this thesis in the years following pointed directly at the matter of the church's hymnody.

> And where an unsound hymnal or catechism is used, there is a denial of the Confessions. How could we answer to God for the use of heterodox hymnals in our congregations! Is it not mockery when one sings to God what is contrary to His Word? . . . A hymnal is a confessional writing in a special sense of the word. When a congregation sings a heterodox song, it confesses false doctrine, even though the congregation pledges adherence to the Unaltered Augsburg Confession in its constitution.[50]

Concerning the matter of the various hymnbooks in use among American Lutherans, the Synodical Conference pointed out a distinction between the hymnal of the Pennsylvania Ministerium[51] and the hymnbooks prepared for use in congregations that united Lutherans and Reformed.[52]

There is also another difference between the "Pennsylvania" hymnal and the "Common Hymnbook." The first may be permitted to be used for a time under protest if the congregation promises to discontinue its use; the "Common Hymnbook" must not be permitted to be used at all, for by using it one would publicly acknowledge membership in the union, as the title implies. When using hymnals which carry the name Lutheran, ignorant Christians will indeed have difficulty understanding the true situation. But it should be remembered that the "Common Hymnbook" may now also be purchased with a "Lutheran" title-page. If a congregation proves obstinate in this matter, it must finally be excluded.[53]

It was clear that the Synodical Conference took its hymnody seriously. However, no effort was made to unite the Synodical Conference in matters of hymnody until 1929 when, at a convention of the Missouri Synod, the matter of revising the *Evangelical Lutheran Hymn-Book* of 1912 was brought to the attention of that body.[54] The convention of the Missouri Synod authorized a revision of the 1912 book with the stipulation that the other members of the Synodical Conference be invited to cooperate in a revision in order that the final result might be a common English hymnbook for that federation.[55]

The other members of the Synodical Conference reacted favorably to this plan and an Intersynodical Committee on Hymnology and Liturgics was organized on January 3, 1930. Prof. W. G. Polack was chosen chairman with Mr. Bernard Schumacher as secretary.[56] The committee studied hymns of English and American origin by non-Lutheran authors, together with hymns of German, Scandinavian, ancient, medieval, and American Lutheran origin. The following principles were accepted by the committee as guides in their work: hymns must be of intrinsic value as to contents and be distinctly Christian; translations must be of good form and in idiomatic English; tunes must be suited to the texts and must be good church music.[57]

The Intersynodical Committee reported periodically over the next decade,[58] and the results of their efforts appeared in 1941 as *The Lutheran Hymnal*,[59] containing 644 hymns, 16 spiritual songs, a number of canticles and chants, together with various orders of service. The work of the editorial committee

> covered a wide field in search of hymns suitable for inclusion in *The Lutheran Hymnal* without losing sight of the fact that the hymnal must be thoroughly *Lutheran* in content. It goes without saying that purity of doctrine was the first and foremost concern, and a goodly number of hymns which were altered in the process of editing were altered in the interest of doctrinal soundness.[60]

The Lutheran Hymnal presented the heritage of Lutheran Reformation hymnody, both in the translations of the texts and in the continued adherence to the rhythmic form of the chorale melodies, to a degree not found among the other Lutheran hymnbooks of its time. In addition, the heritage of Scandinavian hymnody—particularly Norwegian hymnody—and Slovak hymnody was represented to a significantly greater degree than, for example, the *Common Service Book and Hymnal* of 1917. As a treasury of that normative core of Reformation hymnody of the 16th century, *The Lutheran Hymnal* was without equal among American Lutheran hymnbooks in the middle of the 20th century.

The Lutheran Hymnal was quickly adopted by the congregations of the Synodical Conference. By the middle of the century it was the hymnbook being used by approximately one-third of American Lutheranism.

The *Service Book and Hymnal* of 1958

The decade immediately prior to the middle of the 20th century found American Lutheranism divided roughly into

168

three nearly equal groups: the United Lutheran Church in America; the Lutheran Church—Missouri Synod and its associates in the Synodical Conference; and a cluster of smaller independent church bodies with Danish, Swedish, German, Norwegian, and Finnish backgrounds. It was the first and third of these groups, which had united in the National Lutheran Council begun in 1918, which were to join together in preparing a "Common Service Book and Hymnal" that would ultimately appear in 1958.

From the beginning of the 1940s the United Lutheran Church had become engaged in studies that looked forward to the revision of the *Common Service Book and Hymnal* of 1917.[61] At a meeting of the United Lutheran Church in Minneapolis in 1944, the direction of its Common Service Book Committee was altered through a resolution instructing the committee to "seek the fullest possible cooperation with other Lutheran bodies, in the hope of preparing, as nearly as proves feasible, a Common Lutheran Hymnal in America."[62] Upon subsequent invitation, representatives of the American Lutheran Church, the Evangelical Lutheran Church, the Augustana Lutheran Church, and the United Lutheran Church met in Pittsburgh, Pennsylvania, in June 1945 to inaugurate the work. Luther Reed was elected permanent chairman of this Joint Commission and E. E. Ryden was elected secretary. The Lutheran Church—Missouri Synod was not invited to this organizational meeting, and it was not until the following year, when it had been agreed to expand the original scope of the work to include not only a Joint Commission on the Hymnal but a Joint Commission on the Liturgy as well, that the Missouri Synod was also invited to participate. This invitation was subsequently declined because the Missouri Synod had "recently published a new hymnal [and] would not be interested now in effecting another change."[63]

The Evangelical Lutheran Church, largely Norwegian in character, had not forgotten the almost complete absence of Norwegian hymnody from the *Common Service Book and Hymnal* of 1917. Their representatives on the Joint

Commission therefore informed the group that the cooperation of their church body could be secured only if permission were granted to include a selection of additional hymns from *The Lutheran Hymnary* in those copies bound for use in their congregations.[64] From the viewpoint of the Joint Commission such a consideration could only stand in the way of developing a truly "common book." From the viewpoint of the Evangelical Lutheran Church it was a legitimate attempt to preserve their heritage of hymnody before a committee whose chairman, Luther D. Reed, had also headed the group that had virtually excluded the heritage of Scandinavian hymnody from the *Common Service Book and Hymnal* 30 years earlier. Permission was reluctantly granted, but in 1956, the representatives of the Evangelical Lutheran Church on the Joint Commission were finally successful in securing the repeal of this request from their parent body.

The Joint Commission on the Hymnal was guided in its work by the following basic principles:

> The Common Hymnal must be a new work, not simply a conflation of the existing hymnals; it must contain only good hymns providing, as a companion to the liturgy, for the full round of the Christian Year and the Christian Life; the hymns should be devotional rather than didactic or homiletical, and their direction Godward, not manward; the hymnal must be ecumenical in character, expressing the continuity and catholicity of the life of the Church; the final criterion is not Lutheran authorship, but agreement with the teachings of the Word of God; the hymnal must have the highest standards of literary excellence, and each hymn, being an act of worship, should be exalted in language, noble in thought, and reverent in feeling.[65]

By 1958 the work of both the Joint Commissions on the Hymnal and the Liturgy had been completed and the fruits of their efforts appeared in March 1958 as the *Service Book and Hymnal*,[66] published jointly by the eight church bodies that cooperated in its preparation: the American Evangelical

Lutheran Church, the American Lutheran Church, the Augustana Evangelical Lutheran Church, the Evangelical Lutheran Church, the Finnish Evangelical Lutheran Church in America, the Lutheran Free Church, the United Evangelical Lutheran Church, and the United Lutheran Church in America. With the publication of this hymnbook, approximately two-thirds of American Lutheranism was united about a single hymnbook. The remaining one-third consisted of The Lutheran Church—Missouri Synod and the other members of the Synodical Conference who were using *The Lutheran Hymnal* of 1941.

The *Service Book and Hymnal* was not, however, hailed with unanimous approval among the participating groups. Among the Danes, for example, J. C. Aaberg, one of the members of the committee which had produced the *Hymnal for Church and Home,* complained that it contained "more hymns from Catholic sources than from the land of Luther."[67] The same year the *Service Book and Hymnal* appeared, the synod meeting of the Danish Church recommended publication of a supplement of 50 Danish hymns not included in the new book. It appeared in 1960 with only 28 hymns.

It is interesting to note that in setting up the principle guidelines affecting the choice of hymns for the *Service Book and Hymnal,* the Joint Commission could do so without specific reference to the historic confessional heritage of Lutheran hymnody. Moreover, in adopting the view that the hymnody in this collection "should be devotional rather than didactic or homiletical," the Joint Commission departed quite radically from a distinctly Lutheran view of the place of hymnody in the life of the Church.[68]

The emphasis on the "devotional" in hymnody, on "standards of literary excellence" and its relation to the matter of translations, together with the personal proclivities of the various members of the commission, all worked together to exclude almost entirely that normative core of Reformation hymnody from the 16th century together with many of the excellent contributions from the Scandinavian heritage which had their roots in German hymnody. Regarding the matter of translations, the committee reflected essentially the same views that had been voiced by Frederick Bird in connection with the General Council's *Church Book* of 1868, and which had also found a hearing in the preparation of the *Common Service Book and Hymnal* of 1917. One need only compare Bird's views with the concerns regarding translations voiced in the *Introduction* to the Common Hymnal.

> One of the most difficult problems was the application of this final principle [that of literary excellence], especially to hymns of our own heritage where pressure was great for their inclusion. Inferior translations have been accepted in the past because of the affection felt for the original, or because of a majestic chorale tune with which the original was associated. What is often forgotten, or perhaps charitably overlooked, is the fact that a translation seldom succeeds in recreating either the poetic beauty or depth of message of the original.[69]

The result was a hymnbook largely Anglican in orientation and leaning that restored a larger number of the Greek and Latin hymns of the early Church than any other American Lutheran hymnbook, but which also omitted the greatest part of that normative core of Lutheran hymnody from the 16th century, and whose selection from the heritage of the Scandinavian countries was colored by an overly-large infusion of the pietistic songs of the latter 19th century.

As with the *Common Service Book and Hymnal* of 1917, the *Service Book and Hymnal* of 1958 coupled a generally excellent liturgical section with a hymnbook which, while it achieved almost immediately the most widespread use of any American Lutheran hymnal in history, was nevertheless still short of a strongly confessional Lutheran emphasis. While Muhlenberg's dream of "one Church and one book" was closer to being achieved than ever before, this accomplishment, as far as the hymnbook was concerned, was to a large degree still one of form rather than content.

By the early 1960s the eight Lutheran church bodies which had cooperated in the *Service Book and Hymnal* had merged into two larger groups: The American Lutheran Church, formed in 1960, and the Lutheran Church in America, formed in 1962.

The *Lutheran Book of Worship* (1978) and *Lutheran Worship* (1982)

By the beginning of the 1960s there were two Lutheran hymnbooks serving the vast majority of Lutherans in America. The *Service Book and Hymnal* of 1958 served the Lutheran Church in America and the American Lutheran Church; *The Lutheran Hymnal* of 1941 served the Lutheran Church—Missouri Synod and those groups which had been associated with it in the Synodical Conference.

As early as 1956, however, the Missouri Synod had been considering a revision of *The Lutheran Hymnal*, then only 15 years old. Through the late 1950s and early 1960s considerable work had been done on a unilateral revision, and in their report to the Detroit Convention in 1965, the Commission on Worship, Liturgics, and Hymnology presented a recommendation to publish the revision of *The Lutheran Hymnal* in four editions: a tune-text edition, an organist's edition, a keyboard edition, and a choir edition.[70]

However, in the years preceding 1965, the Missouri Synod had begun to take a stance of somewhat greater openness toward other Lutherans, and by the time of the 1965 convention the time seemed ripe to encourage a more cooperative approach to the matter of the revision of *The Lutheran Hymnal*.[71] Instead of approving the original recommendation of its Commission on Worship to proceed with its unilateral revision as originally envisioned, the convention resolved instead:

That we authorize the President in conjunction with the

Vice-Presidents to appoint representatives to pursue a cooperative venture with other Lutheran bodies as soon as possible in working toward, under a single cover:

a) a common liturgical section in rite, rubric, and music;
b) a common core of hymn texts and musical settings; and
c) a variant selection of hymns, if necessary; and be it further

Resolved, That we pledge our joy, willingness, and confidence to the other Lutheran bodies as work in this cooperative project begins.[72]

As a result, invitations were sent by Oliver Harms, president of the Missouri Synod, to various Lutheran church bodies, six of which sent representatives or observers to a meeting in Chicago, Illinois on February 10–11, 1966, of the Inter-Lutheran Consultation on Worship.[73] Out of this meeting was born the Inter-Lutheran Commission on Worship (ILCW) which met for the first time in Chicago, Illinois, November 29–30, 1966.[74]

As the ILCW met to determine its course of action, the representatives of the Lutheran Church in America and The American Lutheran Church could bring to the table the *Service Book and Hymnal*, not yet a decade old. Representatives of the Missouri Synod could bring *The Lutheran Hymnal*, which, however, had been produced almost a quarter-century earlier. With the blessing and approval of the ILCW, the Missouri Synod was encouraged to make available some of the materials which it had been preparing in connection with its—now aban-doned—unilateral revision of *The Lutheran Hymnal*. This material was published in 1969 as *Worship Supplement*[75] and represented the more recently prepared material from the Missouri Synod.

Among the materials prepared by the ILCW was a series of booklets entitled Contemporary Worship, which contained a variety of experimental materials for congregational use. Among these were two small collections of hymns: *Contemporary Worship 1: Hymns* (1969), containing 21 hymns, five from *Worship Supplement* ; and *Contemporary Worship 4: Hymns for Baptism and Holy Communion* (1972), containing 30 hymns, 4 of which were from *Worship Supplement*. In addition a series of music and worship workshops conducted each summer during the decade of preparation of the new hymnbook helped introduce a large number of pastors and church musicians to the features of the new book as they were being developed.

By the summer of 1977 the Lutheran Church in America, the American Lutheran Church, and the Evangelical Lutheran Church of Canada had approved the proposals of the ILCW and had officially authorized the publication of the new hymnbook. That same summer, however, at the convention of the Missouri Synod in Dallas, Texas, that church body took a turn away from cooperative work on the hymnal. Beginning already in 1969, with the election of a decidedly more conservative synodical president and the ensuing years of theological turmoil in the Missouri Synod, voices began to be raised questioning the entire cooperative project that had been begun at the Missouri Synod's initiative in 1965. In response to criticisms of the cooperative venture, the convention of the Missouri Synod in the summer of 1977, rather than approving the collection, as had the other participating Lutheran bodies, called for the appointment of a so-called "Blue-Ribbon Committee" to study the proposed book and recommend one of three options:

> 1) to adopt the final draft of *Lutheran Book of Worship* as presented by the ILCW;
> 2) to adopt the *Lutheran Book of Worship* with particular modifications;
> 3) to reject the *Lutheran Book of Worship* and proceed with the development of a separate new hymnal.

In the wake of this about-face on the part of the Missouri Synod, the Inter-Lutheran Commission on Worship, together with the participating churches which had already approved the new book, decided to proceed with publication.

The following year—1978—saw the publication of *Lutheran Book of Worship*[76] by the participating churches, the Lutheran Church in America, The American Lutheran Church, and the Evangelical Lutheran Church of Canada, but without the Lutheran Church—Missouri Synod. The title page was careful to note, however, that *Lutheran Book of Worship* was "Prepared by the churches participating in the Inter-Lutheran Commission on Worship," and included The Lutheran Church—Missouri Synod among those churches participating in its preparation. The collection contained 569 hymns and canticles. Project director for *Lutheran Book of Worship* was Eugene L. Brand who served in that capacity from 1976–78; the music editor was Richard Hillert. The hymnbook was soon adopted by most congregations. In 1987, just nine years after its publication, the Lutheran Church in America and The American Lutheran Church merged to form the Evangelical Lutheran Church in America.

The issuance of the report of the Special Hymnal Review Committee of the Missouri Synod[77] in May 1978 heralded the demise of any hopes for the adoption of *Lutheran Book of Worship* in the Missouri Synod. The recommendation of the committee was that "the Synod consider using a revised edition of *Lutheran Book of Worship*."[78] The subsequent decision of the Missouri Synod at its 1979 convention in St. Louis, Missouri, was to adopt its revision of *Lutheran Book of Worship*—to be called *Lutheran Worship* when completed—as an official hymnal of the Missouri Synod. In so doing it was essentially following the second of the three options suggested by the 1977 convention, to adopt the *Lutheran Book of Worship*, but with modifications that it felt were necessary. Three years later, in December of 1982, *Lutheran Worship*[79] appeared, a collection of 520 hymns, canticles, and chants. Fred L. Precht, executive secretary of the Commission on Worship, was the general editor of the book. Paul Bunjes was the music editor.

In spite of several significant differences, the many similarities between the two books were striking. Two of the three settings for Holy Communion were virtually identical, a greater emphasis on holy baptism was evident throughout both books, and both placed a great emphasis on the singing of the Psalms by the congregation and provided musical vehicles for that purpose. As far as the hymnody of the two collections was concerned, both included a significant number of hymns from that normative core of Reformation hymnody, and for the first time in American Lutheranism, both books provided an official place for the Hymn of the Day in the Eucharistic liturgy and provided a listing of the appointed *de tempore* hymns throughout the church year. Among the significant attendant books provided for each book of worship were the *Hymnal Companion to the Lutheran Book of Worship* and the *Lutheran Worship: Hymnal Companion*.[80]

One question remained to be answered. Much of the criticism contained in the Report of the Special Hymnal Review Committee centered around allegations of false doctrine in *Lutheran Book of Worship*. Since the Constitution of the Missouri Synod stated that a condition of membership is the "exclusive use of doctrinally pure agenda [and] hymnbooks. . ." (Art. VI, par. 4), it was inevitable that the Commission on Constitutional Matters would be asked to rule whether use of the *Lutheran Book of Worship* was a violation of the Synod's Constitution. In an Official Notice published the year after the appearance of *Lutheran Worship*, the Commission replied to just such an inquiry as follows:

> If in fact the *Lutheran Book of Worship* is not "doctrinally pure," then under Article VI of our Synod's Constitution it should not be used by our congregations. However, we can find no evidence of an official decision on the part of the convention of the Synod itself that the *Lutheran Book of Worship* is doctrinally impure.[81]

Thus congregations of the Missouri Synod, a significant number of which were already using *Lutheran Book of Worship* were declared not in violation of the Synod's

Constitution. This created a situation in which congregations were free to adopt either *Lutheran Book of Worship*, *Lutheran Worship*, or opt to remain using *The Lutheran Hymnal*.

In 1965 Muhlenberg's dream of "one church, one book" seemed within the grasp of America's Lutherans. But by the end of the century there were still two books serving the majority of Lutherans in America, the *Lutheran Book of Worship* and *Lutheran Worship*. Yet, as a result of one of the ironies of history, those two books were closer together in both content and spirit than the two books which they were replacing, *The Lutheran Hymnal* and the *Service Book and Hymnal*. Both new books stood for and provided materials for a richer liturgical life in the congregation, and both contained as rich a treasury of Reformation hymnody as American Lutheranism had yet seen.

The Wisconsin Evangelical Lutheran Synod and *Christian Worship: A Lutheran Hymnal* (1993)

One additional development in the last decade of the 20th century completes the picture of Lutheran hymnody in America, the appearance in 1993 of *Christian Worship: A Lutheran Hymnal*, the product of the Wisconsin Evangelical Lutheran Synod. While hardly the result of consolidation and consensus, this last American Lutheran hymnal to be published in the 20th century marks the hymnological coming of age of a conservative Lutheran church body whose history of congregational song had largely been tied to its partners in the Synodical Conference.

The Wisconsin Evangelical Lutheran Synod was first organized in 1892 as the Joint Evangelical Lutheran Synod of Wisconsin, Minnesota, Michigan, and Other States, an amalgamation of the synods listed in its title.[82] While its present membership stands at well over 400,000 and is the third largest Lutheran church body in America, its early membership was made up largely of a relatively small number of Pommeranians and Brandenburgers who had come in the emigrations from Germany in the 1830s and 1840s. As with other immigrant groups, they brought with them their hymnals from the homeland with predictably confusing results. In addition to the German-language books the immigrants brought with them, "there were a number of congregations of the Wisconsin Synod who ordered both standard and customized German-language hymnals from both Germany and America."[83] Some congregations may have used Demme's *Deutsches Gesangbuch* of the Pennsylvania Ministerium, others the Missouri Synod's *Kirchengesangbuch* of 1847. Overtures were made to the Pennsylvania, New York, and the Ohio Synod at various times regarding the possibility of revising or using their hymnbooks, but nothing came of them.[84]

The Wisconsin Synod had been a member of the General Council at its inception in 1867, but left in 1869 in disagreement over the Four Points. Therefore the General Council's *Church Book* of 1868 was not available to it, and in 1869 the Wisconsin Synod determined to publish its own German collection, presenting to its 1870 convention a hymnbook published by George Brumder, brother-in-law of the past Synod President Streissguth. The Synod gave Brumder a 30-year contract to publish the hymnbook and was to receive "a payment of five cents for every copy sold by the firm."[85] Certain changes were requested by the synod,[86] and the hymnbook finally appeared in 1872 as the *Evang.-Lutherisches Gesangbuch fuer Kirche, Schule und Haus*,[87] containing 695 hymns. It continued to be printed as late as the 1930s.

Two English hymnals were also produced by the Wisconsin Synod: the *Church Hymnal for Lutheran Services*, produced sometime around 1905,[88] containing words for 115 hymns. and a second English hymnbook, the *Book of Hymns for the Evangelical Lutheran Joint Synod of Wisconsin and Other States*, published in 1917, and largely the work of Pastor Otto Hagedorn of Milwaukee. About 1926 there was consideration of producing an Addendum to the *Book of Hymns*, but nothing came of it.[89] As early as 1925, however, thought had been given to the possibility of an inter-synodical hymnal for the members of the Synodical Conference. By 1929 the Missouri Synod had established a committee to meet with representatives of the sister synods of the Synodical Conference for just that purpose. The Wisconsin Synod participated in that process and when *The Lutheran Hymnal* was published in 1941 as a joint project of the Synodical Conference, it provided the Wisconsin Synod with a hymnal it was to use until the 1990s. In 1963 the Wisconsin Synod and the Evangelical Lutheran Synod (the "Little Norwegian Synod") withdrew from the Synodical Conference over doctrinal matters, ultimately resulting in the dissolution of the Synodical Conference in 1967.

The Missouri Synod, meanwhile, had initiated work in 1953 on a revision of *The Lutheran Hymnal*. In 1959 the Wisconsin Synod accepted the invitation to share in the revision work. However, the Missouri Synod, in 1965, abandoned this unilateral revision and invited other Lutherans to join in preparing a common hymnal, work that ultimately led to the publication of *Lutheran Book of Worship* and *Lutheran Worship*. Representatives of the Wisconsin Evangelical Lutheran Synod were in attendance as observers at the Chicago meeting of the Inter-Lutheran Commission on Worship[90] and continued to participate as observers as they were able. After the Missouri Synod had determined to produce its own revision of *Lutheran Book of Worship*, information regarding the new project continued to be shared with representatives of the Wisconsin Synod in the hope that they might become involved in the work leading to *Lutheran Worship*.

In 1983, however, one year after the appearance of *Lutheran Worship*, the Wisconsin Synod in its convention resolved:

> That the Synod now begin work on a new/revised hymnal of its own, one that under the blessings of God will be scripturally sound and edifying, welcomed and

judged to be highly satisfactory by a majority of our members, in harmony with the character and heritage of our church body, and reflecting the larger perspective and mainstream of the worship of the Christian church.

The new book appeared in 1993 as *Christian Worship: A Lutheran Hymnal*. [91] It was introduced together with *Christian Worship: Accompaniment for Liturgy and Psalms* and *Christian Worship: Manual*.[92] The Hymnal Project Director was Rev. Kurt J. Eggert and the Hymnal Project Music Editor was Kermit G. Moldenhauer. The hymnbook contains 623 hymns, 59 psalm settings with refrains, and a variety of liturgical material. Of the 623 hymns, over 400 are taken—with some changes in language—from *The Lutheran Hymnal*. As a result, the heritage of Reformation congregational song is just as strongly represented in *Christian Worship: A Lutheran Hymnal* as in either *Lutheran Book of Worship* or *Lutheran Worship*.

Afterword

Born of the desire that God would be praised and his Word proclaimed to all the earth through the vehicle of a liturgically-centered congregational song, the focus of hymnody in the Lutheran tradition has faced a variety of challenges since the early days of the Reformation. It will undoubtedly face new tests and challenges in the years to come. The chief arena for those tests and challenges has been the succession of hymnals that Lutherans have produced.

For almost four and one-half centuries Lutheran hymnody has changed and adapted with each successive age, absorbing what it has found useful and edifying in each successive age, rejecting that song which it has found to be contrary to its liturgical, sacramental understanding of worship. Each successive hymnal that Lutherans have produced has been the potential point of conflict where the spirit of the Lutheran tradition meets the spirit of the age. Where those two spirits have largely coincided there has been one result; where they are at cross purposes, quite another outcome occurs.

Central to this conflict has been the attitude toward that normative core of Lutheran hymnody developed early in the Reformation in such collections as the Babst hymnbook of 1545. This brief overview demonstrates that where Lutherans have been faithful to a Lutheran understanding of the role of music and hymnody in the life and worship of the church, they have sought to embrace that normative core of congregational song birthed by the Reformation.

Where that Reformation song was alive and well in the mouths and hearts of congregations, there was the assurance that the Gospel message of sin and grace, death and rebirth, would continue to resound within the church. Where that normative core was diluted, emasculated, or eliminated from Lutheran hymnbooks, it was a muted message—often a message other than the Gospel—that was to sound out. Through the centuries the church's song has continued to be enriched with the best of the new song of each successive age. But where the church has lost its moorings in the Gospel proclamation so uniquely given expression in the 16th-century chorale, the church's worship has experienced deterioration, decay, and decline.

Johann Walter, Luther's friend and musical adviser, in his "In Praise of the Noble Art of Music" explains why God supplied music as a gift to us for use in his praise and in the proclamation of his Word:

> That such unmerited free grace
> (Which God from love for all our race
> Had promised in His Word) might be
> Kept fresh in human memory
> And move the heart to high delight
> In praising God both day and night—
> *This* is the weightiest reason why
> God music did at once supply.

A Lutheran understanding of music—and hymnody—in worship is just this: to keep fresh in human memory the unmerited free grace God promises in his Word, and to move our hearts to high delight in praising God. And that is what the Lutheran chorale does with unique grace and splendor—keeping the message of the Gospel fresh in our memory. Where that goal is kept in mind, fostered and encouraged, the chorale lives and flourishes in congregational life.

The process of sifting through the new material of each successive age is part of the hymnbook-making enterprise. Traditionally conservative by nature, the process of hymnbook-making has proven to be a blessed impediment standing in the way of the adoption of every passing textual and musical fad or fancy. This "cultural lag" which, to some extent, can be seen in every hymnbook, and which is criticized by some as an example of the continuing irrelevance of the church, makes possible that very sifting process that attempts to ensure that the treasury of the church's song placed into the hands of the believers does, in fact, reflect in a faithful way the beliefs and convictions of the church.

The challenges to American Lutheran hymnody in the past several centuries, however, do not die easily. Pietism, rationalism, revivalism, and an easy-going ecumenism have reappeared in the 20th century in new and tempting guises. Marketed and promoted with all the trappings of 20th-century technology, they continue to threaten to move Lutheran hymnody from its central concerns of proclamation and praise to other attractive, but peripheral, concerns. Rather than an assurance mediated through God's Word and sacraments, a new pietism has arisen in our time that seeks religious assurance within one's self, that seeks immediate affirmation in the senses. Rather than texts which "tell the story," we are bombarded with songs that, at best, reflect only a bumper-sticker theology. Musically, the church is awash in a triviality designed either to make us feel good or to manipulate us to someone else's predetermined ends. That triviality makes a mockery of the integrity of the Gospel itself.

While we cannot foretell the outcome for the foreseeable future, we know that the good and gracious will of our God, who is ultimately in control, will prevail.

Notes

Preface
(pp.13–19)

1. Henry Melchior Muhlenberg, *The Journals of Henry Melchior Muhlenberg*, 3 vols. trans. T. G. Tappert and J. W. Doberstein (Philadelphia: Muhlenberg Press, 1942–1958), I:221. Hereafter *Journals*.

2. Quoted in R. Harold Terry, "Lutheran Hymnody in North America," *Hymnal Companion to the Lutheran Book of Worship*, Marilyn Stulken, ed. Philadelphia: Fortress Press, 1981, p. 82.

3. From the Preface to the *Erbauliche Liedersammlung*, 1786. Unless otherwise indicated, translations from other than English-language hymnbooks are by the author.

4. Edwin Scott Gaustad, *Historical Atlas of Religion in America* (New York & Evanston: Harper and Row, Publishers, 1962), p. 18–19.

Chapter 1: The Background of the 16th-Century Lutheran Reformatiion
(pp.21–29)

1. Martin Luther, *Works*. American edition. Ed. by Jaroslav Pelikan and Helmut Lehmann (St. Louis: Concordia Publishing House; Philadelphia: Fortress Publishing House, 1955–). 55 vols. 53: 191. Hereafter LW.

2. See Bard Thompson, *Liturgies of the Western Church* (Cleveland and New York: The World Publishing Company, 1961), p. 104. The other two being the prominence given to preaching and the restoration to the people of communion in both kinds.

3. Friedrich Blume, *Protestant Church Music*. (New York: W. W. Norton & Company Inc., 1974), p. 48. Originally publised as *Geschichte der evangelischen Kirchenmusik* (Kassel: Baeren-reiter Verlag, 1964).

4. LW 53:36.

5. LW 53:68–69.

6. For a listing of some of these broadsheets see *D. Martin Luthers Werke. Kritische Gesamtausgabe* (Weimar: H. Boehlau, 1883–), 35:375–377. Hereafter WA. Leupold notes that "A chronicler of the city of Magdeburg gives a vivid account of a peddler who on May 6, 1524, sang the new Lutheran hymns on the market place and sold the leaflets to the people. The mayor had him clapped in jail, but the enthusiastic burghers saw that he was freed in short order to continue singing the hymns of Martin Luther." LW 53:191.

7. LW 53:192.

8. A description of these hymnals may be found in WA 35: 320, 325, 327–330, 332–334, 346–357, 362–366.

9. Edwin Liemohn, *The Chorale Through Four Hundred Years of Musical Development as a Congregational Hymn* (Philadelphia: Muhlenberg Press, 1953), p. 28.

10. *Geistliche Lieder*. Mit einer newen vorrhede D. Mart. Luth. Leipzig, 1545. Facsimile, Baerenreiter Verlag zu Kassel, 1929.

11. Johann Daniel von der Heydt, *Geschichte der Evangelischen Kirchenmusik in Deutschland*. 2. Auflage (Berlin: Trowitzsch & Sohn, 1932), p. 54.

12. LW 53:194.

13. LW 53:332.

14. The text of Luther's Preface to the Babst hymnal can be found in LW 53:332–334.

15. LW 53:332.

16. Blume, *Protestant Church Music*, p. 48.

17. A comparison of a representative selection of hymns from the Babst hymnbook with their appearance or non-appearance in the various Lutheran hymnbooks used in America provides an interesting reflection of how this body of hymnody—considered to be normative for Lutheran congregational song in the 16th century—fared in the succeeding periods of American Lutheran history. A chart showing this comparison as well as a listing of the specific texts from the Babst hymnbook used in this

comparison may be found in Appendix A.

18. Ibid., p.34f.

19. Liemohn, *The Chorale*, p. 31.

20. Joel Lundeen, "Scandinavian Hymnody: Sweden," *Hymnal Companion to the Lutheran Book of Worship*. Marilyn Kay Stulken, ed. (Philadelphia: Fortress Press, 1981), p. 47.

21. For a reprint of this collection, omitting the melody line, see *Remains of Coverdale*. Edited for the Parker Society by Rev. George Pearson (Cambridge: The University Press, 1846), vol. 14, p. 533f.

22. Kenneth R. Long, *The Music of the English Church* (New York: St. Martin's Press, 1971), p. 27.

23. Ibid.

Chapter 2: Early Evidence of Lutheran Hymnody in America
(pp.31-37)

1. See Carlton York Smith, *Early Lutheran Hymnody in America. From the Colonial Period to the Year 1850*. diss., University of Southern California, 1956, p. 7f.

2. The first specific mention of Lutherans among the Dutch settlers is in 1643 by a Catholic missionary to the Indians who mentions Lutherans as among other groups besides Calvinists in the colony. See William J. Finck, *Lutheran Landmarks and Pioneers in America* (Philadelphia: The United Lutheran Publication House, 1913), p. 22–23. Smith, *Early Lutheran Hymnody in America*, notes that while there is no specific mention of Lutherans among the early Dutch settlers, the Lutheran Church in Amsterdam had a membership of some 30,000 at this time and it would have been probable that some Lutherans found their way in this group.

3. Harry J. Kreider, *History of the United Lutheran Synod of New York and New England* (Philadelphia: Muhlenberg Press, 1954). pp. 1–2.

4. Arnold J. H. van Laer., trans., "The Lutheran Church in New York, 1649–1772. Records in the Lutheran Church Archives at Amsterdam, Holland," *Bulletin of the New York Public Library*, 49:4, 1945.

5. Simon Hart and Harry J. Kreider, trans., "The Lutheran Church in New York, 1649–1772. Records in the Lutheran Church Archives at Amsterdam, Holland," *Bulletin of the New York Public Library*, 50:835, 1946.

6. See Edward Christopher Wolf, *Lutheran Church Music in America During the Eighteenth and Early Nineteenth Centuries.* diss., University of Illinois, 1960; also Smith, *Early Lutheran Hymnody in America.*

7. Amandus Johnson, *The Swedish Settlements on the Delaware, 1635–1664,* cited in *Church Music and Musical Life in Pennsylvania in the Eighteenth Century* (Philadelphia: Printed for the Society, 1926) Vol. I, pp. 187–188.

8. Decius' setting of the Gloria was the popular 16th-century hymn "Allein Gott in der Hoeh sei Ehr." Luther's setting of the Creed was his "Wir glauben all an einen Gott."

9. Wolf, *Lutheran Church Music in America*, p. 23

10. Ibid., p. 34.

Chapter 3: The First Lutheran Hymnbook and Chorale Book in America
(pp. 39–50)

1. For an orientation to the growth of Lutheranism in the colonies, see Gaustad, *Historical Atlas of Religion*, pp. 16–19.

2. See Theodore G. Tappert, "The Influence of Pietism in Colonial American Lutheranism," in F. Earnest Stoeffler, *Continental Pietism and Early American Christianity* (Grand Rapids: Wm. B. Eerdmans Publishing Co., 1976), p. 13f. For representative writings of Continental Pietist authors, see Peter C. Erb, ed., *Pietists: Selected Writings* (New York: Paulist Press, 1983), part of the series Classics of Western Spirituality.

3. For a general introduction to German Lutheran hymnody see the following: Carl Schalk, "German Hymnody," in *Hymnal Companion to the Lutheran Book of Worship*, Marilyn Kay Stulken, ed. (Philadelphia: Fortress Press, 1981), pp. 19–33; Carl Schalk, "German Church Song," in *The Hymnal 1982 Companion*, Raymond F. Glover, ed. (New York: The Church Hymnal Corporation, 1990), pp. 288–309.

4. Wilhelm Nelle, *Geschichte des deutschen evangelischen Kirchen liedes* (Vierte unveraenderte Auflage; Hildesheim: Georg Olms Verlagsbuchhandlung, 1962), p. 200.

5. Johann August Spitta, *Johann Sebastian Bach* (London: Novello and Co., 1899), I, 362–363.

6. Liemohn, *The Chorale*, p. 65.

7. Friedrich Blume, *Protestant Church Music* (New York: W. W. Norton & Co., 1974), p. 260. Originally published as *Geschichte der evangelischen Kirchenmusik*, Baerenreiter Verlag, 1964.

8. Ibid., p. 262.

9. Johann Anastasii Freylinghausen, *Geistreiches Gesangbuch*, Der Kern Alter und Neuer Lieder, Wie auch die Noten der unbekennten Melodeyen Und darzu gehoerige mitzliche Register in sich haltend . . . (Halle: Gedruckt und verlegt im Waeysenhause, 1704). This book contained 683 hymns with 174 melodies. The music consisted of melody with figured bass.

10. *Neues Geistreiches Gesangbuch*, auserlesene, so Alte als Neue, geistliche und liebliche Lieder, nebst den Noten der unbekanten Melodeyen, in sich haltend, Zur Erweckung heiliger Andacht und Erbauung im Glauben und gottseligen Wegen (Halle: Gedruckt und verlegt im Waysenhause, 1714). This hymnal contained 815 hymns with 158 melodies with figured bass.

11. Johann Anastasii Freylinghausen, *Geistreiches Gesangbuch*, den Kern alter und neuer Lieder in sich verhaltend: Jetzo von neuen so eingerichtet, Dasz alle Gesaenge, so in den vorhin unter diesem Namen alhier herausgekommenen Gesangbuecher befindlich, unter ihre Rubriquen zusammengebracht, auch die Noten aller alten und neuen Melodeyen beygefueget worden, und mit einem Vorbericht herausgegeben von Gotthilf August Francken (Halle: in Verlegung des Waeysenhauses, 1741).

12. The edition of 1771 contains 1581 hymns as in the edition of 1741. The differences in this edition are minor and are noted in Johannes Zahn, *Die Melodien der deutschen evangelischen Kirchenlieder* aus den Quellen geschoepft und mitgeteilt (Reprografischer Nachdruck der Ausgabe Guetersloh 1893; Hildesheim: Georg Olms Verlagsbuchhandlung, 1963), V, 353.

13. Muhlenberg, *Journals*, I, 49.

14. For an older standard biography of Muhlenberg see William J. Mann, *The Life and Times of Henry Melchior Muhlenberg* (Philadelphia: G. W. Frederick, 1887). A more recent treatment may be found in Leonard R.

Riforgiato, *Missionary of Moderation: Henry Melchior Muhlenberg and the Lutheran Church in English America* (Lewisburg, Pa.: Bucknell University press, 1980). For brief biographical sketches of Muhlenberg and the more important members of his family see Erwin L. Lueker, (ed.), *Lutheran Cyclopedia*. rev. ed. (St. Louis: Concordia Publishing House, 1975), pp. 559ff.

15. Abdel Ross Wentz, *A Basic History of Lutheranism in America* (Philadelphia: Muhlenberg Press, 1955), p. 17.

16. Halle, it might be pointed out, was less than twenty miles from Leipzig where Johann Sebastian Bach served (1723–1750) during Muhlenberg's term as teacher at the Halle Orphanage and for almost a decade after Muhlenberg came to America.

17. Muhlenberg, *Journals*, I:607, 434ff.; II:83. This hymnal which, in various European editions, was widely used by the Germans throughout the colonies, was also printed in an American edition in Germantown by Christopher Sauer. Luther Reed, *The Lutheran Liturgy*. rev. ed. (Philadelphia: Fortress Press, 1947, pp. 166–167, gives 1762 as the date of this American edition, while E. E. Ryden gives the date as 1759 ("Hymnbook," *The Encyclopedia of the Lutheran Church*, Julius Bodensieck, ed. (Minneapolis: Augsburg Publishing House, 1965), pp. 1072–1090. Edward C. Wolf, "Lutheran Hymnody and Music Published in America 1700–1850: A Descriptive Bibliography," *Concordia Historical Institute Quarterly* (Vol. 50, N. 4, Winter 1977), p.165ff., gives 1757 as the date of the first edition.

18. Muhlenberg, *Journals*, I 607; III, 339, 524–25.

19. Liemohn, *The Chorale*, p. 135.

20. Ibid. This book was used by the Salzburgers who settled in South Carolina.

21. See Muhlenberg, *Journals*, I, 9, 421, 653; II:31, 433, 525, 552, 597; III: 4, 339, 524–25.

22. See David Christian, *Henry Melchior Muhlenberg's Contribution to Lutheran Worship and Music in America*. MCM thesis, Concordia University, River Forest, Illinois, 1982, for a listing of the approximately 250 different hymn titles mentioned in Muhlenberg's *Journals*.

23. Muhlenberg, *Journals*, I:49.

24. Ibid., II:31.

25. A. Spaeth, H. E. Jacobs, and G. F. Spicker (eds.), *Documentary History of the Evangelical Lutheran Ministerium of Pennsylvania and Adjacent States.* Proceedings of the Annual Convention from 1748 to 1841. Compiled and Translated from Records in the Archives and from the Written Protocols (Philadelphia: Board of Publication of the General Council of the Evangelical Lutheran Church in North America, 1898), p. 183. Hereafter referred to as the *Documentary History*.

26. Ibid., pp 183–184.

27. Muhlenberg, *Journals*, III:497.

28. Muhlenberg, *Journals*, III: 524–525.

29. Ibid.

30. See Appendix B for a comparison of the Tables of Contents for each of these books.

31. *Documentary History*, pp. 189–190.

32. Muhlenberg, *Journals*, III:701.

33. Ibid., III:719–720.

34. *Erbauliche Liedersammlung zum Gottesdienstlichen Gebrauch in den Vereinigten Evangelisch Lutherischen Gemeinen in Nord-America.* Gesamlet, eingerichtet und zum Druck befoerdert durch die gesamten Glieder des hiesigen Vereinigten Evangelisch Lutherischen ministeriums. Erste Auflage. Germantaun. Gedruckt bey Leibert und Billmeyer, 1786.

35. From the Preface to the *Erbauliche Liedersammlung*.

36. "Die Kirchen-Gesangbuecher," *Der Lutheraner*, VII (October 1, 1850), 20. The writer is not identified.

37. J. Nicum, *Geschichte des Evangelisch-Lutherischen Ministerium vom Staate New York und angrenzenden Staaten und Laendern* (Reading, Pa.: Verlag des New York-Ministeriums, 1888), p. 193.

38. *Documentary History*, p. 216.

39. Raymond J. Brunner, *That Ingenious Business: Pennsylvania German Organ Builders* (Birdsboro, Pennsylvania: The Pennsylvania German Society, 1990), p. 230, points out that by 1825 there were probably at least one

hundred organs in Southeastern Pennsylvania alone, and that Lutheran churches were often the first church in a community to obtain an organ.

40. Documentary History, p. 270.

41. Ibid., p. 430.

42. *Choral-Buch fuer die Erbauliche Liedersammlung der Deutschen Evangelisch-Lutherischen Gemeinen in Nord-Amerika* (Philadelphia: Conrad Zentler and Georg Blake, 1813).

Chapter 4: Early Attempts at English and German Hymnals
(pp. 51–65)

1. Gaustad, *Historical Atlas of Religion*, p. 18–19.

2. Muhlenberg, *Journals*, I, 300.

3. Ibid., I, 297. Muhlenberg's reference to the hymn "Jesu, deine tiefe Wunden" is not quite correct. While this is the title of Johann Heermann's great hymn, the English hymnbook to which Muhlenberg refers utilized the altered text from the Hannover Gesangbuch of 1657 which begins "Jesu, deine heilge Wunden."

4. *Psalmodia Germanica: or, The German Psalmody*. Translated from the High Dutch. Together with their proper tunes, and thorough Bass (Third edition, corrected and very much enlarged; London: Reprinted, and sold by H. Gaine, 1756). Included in this hymnbook, beginning with the 1732 edition, was a *Supplement to German Psalmody: Done into English*. Together with their Proper Tunes. and Thorough Bass, for promoting Sacred Harmony in Private Families . . . The 1756 edition was reprinted again in 1765.

5. Benson, *The English Hymn*, p. 410–411.

6. Theodore Emanuel Schmauck, *A History of the Lutheran Church in Pennsylvania (1638–1820)*. From the Original Sources (Lancaster: Pennsylvania-German Society, 1903) I, 180. Schmauck notes that the Royal German St. James Chapel was founded by the husband of Queen Anne, Prince George of Denmark, who was himself a Lutheran. In order to provide services in German, the Royal Chapel had engaged Lutheran chaplains from Germany.

7. From the "Preface" to the *Psalmodia Germanica*.

8. Ibid.

9. Quoted in Stulken, *Hymnal Companion*, p. 91.

10. The sixty chorale tunes listed in a special appendix at the back of the *Psalmodia Germanica*, which were the tunes to which these texts were to be sung, may be found in Wolf, *Lutheran Church Music in America*, p. 54–55.

11. William M. Reynolds, "English Lutheran Hymn Books," *Evangelical Review*, XI (October, 1859), 185.

12. Ibid. The one translation of Jacobi—mixed with translations of some stanzas by Russell and Winkworth—which was to be found in a number of Lutheran hymnals down through the *Service Book and Hymnal* of 1958 was his "God, who madest earth and heaven." All three Lutheran hymnals in present use no longer contain this hymn.

13. Benson, *The English Hymn*, p. 411.

14. Luther D. Reed, *Worship: A Study of Corporate Devotion* (Philadelphia: Fortress Press, 1959), p. 149. Yet the *Service Book and Hymnal* notes the inclusion of something of Jacobi's work (see #205), mixed together with what were presumably loftier translations of greater literary style by Russell and Winkworth.

15. In 1792, the Pennsylvania Ministerium introduced the word "German" into its official name, and by 1805 it had taken action forbidding the use of any language other than German in its synodical sessions.

16. *A Hymn and Prayer-Book: for the use of such Lutheran Churches as use the English Language.* Collected by John C. Kunze, D. D. Senior of the Clergy in the State of New York (New York: Hurtin and Commardinger, 1795).

17. *A collection of hymns for the use of the Protestant Church of the United Brethren* (London: 1789). This hymnbook contained 887 hymns and became the standard hymnbook of the Moravians at that time.

18. From the "Preface" to *A Hymn and Prayer-Book*.

19. *Evangelical Review*, XVI (January 1865), 26. Frederick Mayer Bird (1838—1908) contributed three significant articles on the subject of American Lutheran hymnals which appeared in the *Evangelical Review* in 1865. For a brief biographical sketch of Bird, see Luther D. Reed, *The*

Lutheran Liturgy, rev. ed. (Philadelphia: Fortress Press, 1947), pp. 180—181. He is also the author of the article on "American Hymnody" in Julian's *Dictionary of Hymnology*.

20. Quoted in *Evangelical Review*, XI (October, 1859), 188.

21. Nicum, *Geschichte*, p. 93.

22. *Evangelical Review*, XVI (January, 1865), 29.

23. George Strebeck was brought up a Lutheran in Baltimore, Md., but later became a Methodist preacher. Anxious, so he claimed, for service in the Lutheran Church, he was called as an assistant pastor to Kunze in 1794 and ordained in 1796 by the New York Ministerium. The same year Strebeck became pastor of Zion Church in New York, the first English-speaking Lutheran congregation in America, formed out of Kunze's German congregation. A few years later Strebeck carried the bulk of his congregation over to the Protestant Episcopal Church.

24. Quoted from the "Preface" to *A Collection of evangelical Hymns* in Benson, *The English Hymn*, p. 412.

25. *A Collection of evangelical Hymns, made from different authors and collections, for the Lutheran Church, in New York*. By George Strebeck (New York: John Tiebout), 1797.

26. Benson, *The English Hymn*, pp. 412–413.

27. From the "Preface" to *A collection of evangelical Hymns*.

28. Benson, *The English Hymn*, pp. 412–413.

29. Nicum, *Geschichte*, p. 84.

30. *A choice Selection of evangelical Hymns, from various authors: for the use of the English Evangelical-Lutheran Church in New York*. By Ralph Williston (New York: J. C. Totten, 1806).

31. Benson, *The English Hymn*, p. 413.

32. Lueker, *Lutheran Cyclopedia*, p. 455.

33. *Das Neu eingerichtete Gesangbuch*, bestehend Aus der Sammlung der besten Liedern, zum Gebrauch des oeffentlichen Deutschen Gottesdienst's, und anderen Uebungen zur Gottseligkeit, in den Vereinigten Staaten, von

Nord-America (Erste Auflage: New Market: Gedruckt bey Ambrosius Henkel und Comp., 1810).

34. *Church Hymn Book,* consisting of newly composed Hymns, with an addition of Hymns and Psalms, from other authors, carefully adopted for the use of public worship, and many other occasions. By Paul Henkel, Minister of the Gospel (First edition; New Market, Shenandoah County, Va.: Printed in Solomon Henkel's Printing Office, 1816).

35. Benson, *The English Hymn,* p. 415.

36. Ibid.

37. Henkel, *History of the Tennessee Synod,* p. 69.

38. Benson, *The English Hymn,* p. 415.

Chapter 5: Movements toward Accommodation
(pp.67–92)

1. For a fuller discussion of the influence of rationalism and the spirit of unionism see Wentz, *Basic History of Lutheranism in America,* pp. 73f. Vergilius Ferm, *The Crisis in American Lutheran Theology* (New York: The Century Co., 1927), p. 23, n. 37, notes that already in 1786 with the inclusion of the word "German" in the official name of the Pennsylvania Ministerium, the exodus of "thousands of English-speaking Lutherans into the Episcopal and other Protestant denominations, followed in the wake of this turn in the constitution toward particularism.

For a particularly perceptive comparison and contrast between the liturgies and congregational song of the Lutheran and Reformed traditions in America during this period see Paul Westermeyer, *What Shall We Sing in a Foreign Land? Theology and Cultic Song in the German Reformed and Lutheran Churches of Pennsylvania, 1830–1900* (Ph.D. diss., University of Chicago, 1978).

2. Richard C. Wolf, "The Americanization of the German Lutherans, 1683–1829" (Ph. D. diss., Yale University, 1947), 436–442.

3. Nicum, *Geschichte,* p. 93.

4. The members of the committee cannot be determined with certainty from the minutes of the Ministerium. However, an article on "English

Lutheran Hymnbooks" (*Evangelical Review*, XI, October 1859, p. 188) by William Reynolds states that the committee consisted of F. H. Quitman, Augustus Wackerhagen, and Mayer [undoubtedly P. F. Mayer, pastor of St. John's Lutheran Church in Philadelphia and chairman of a committee which prepared the 1843 edition of this same hymnbook].

5. *A Collection of Hymns, and a Liturgy*, for the use of the Evangelical Lutheran Churches: published by order of the Evangelical Lutheran Synod of the State of New York (New York and Philadelphia, 1814).

6. Augustus Wackerhagen (1774–1865) was pastor of the Lutheran churches in Schoharie and Cobleskill, New York, from 1805–1815. His wife was a sister of P. F. Mayer and a step-daughter of F. H. Quitman. Wackerhagen followed his father-in-law as president of the New York Ministerium, serving from 1826–1829.

7. Nicum, *Geschichte*, p. 93.

8. *Evangelical Review*, XI (October, 1859), 188.

9. From the "Preface" to Quitman's *Collection*.

10. Ibid.

11. Martin E. Marty, *The Infidel: Freethought and American Religion* (Cleveland and New York: Meridian Books, The World Publishing Company, 1961), p. 34.

12. Reed, *The Lutheran Liturgy*, p. 178.

13. *Evangelical Review*, XI (October, 1859), 189.

14. Ibid., p. 190.

15. Ibid., p. 191.

16. Ibid., p. 190.

17. Ibid.

18. Ibid.

19. The *Preface* lists the complete committee as follows: P. F. Mayer, C. R. Demme, F. G. Mayer, F. W. Geissenhainer Jr., and Wm. D. Strobel. The committee was appointed by the 38th Synod of the New York Ministerium

in New York in September, 1833.

20. *Evangelical Review*, XI (October, 1859), 192.

21. Ibid, p. 193.

22. From the *Preface*.

23. Jacob Eckhard, *Choral Book Containing Psalms, Hymns, Anthems and Chants. Used in the Episcopal Churches of Charleston, South Carolina; and a Collection of Tunes, Adapted to the Metres in the Hymn-Book, Published by Order of the Evangelical Lutheran Synod of the State of New York. The Whole a selection for the Service of All Protestant Churches in America.* (Boston: James Loring, [1816]). No date appears on the title page; the date is that of the copyright notice. For additional information see also George W. Williams, *Jacob Eckhard's Choirmaster's Book* of 1809 (Columbia: University of South Carolina Press, 1971).

24. See George W. Williams, "Charleston Church Music, 1562–1833," *Journal of the American Musicological Society*, Vol. VII (Spring, 1954), p. 42. Eckhard had been brought up in the Lutheran Church and had earlier served as organist at St. John's Lutheran Church in Charleston.

25. For a detailed discussion of this collection see Edward C. Wolf, "Peter Erben and America's First Lutheran Tunebook in English," *American Musical Life in Context and Practice to 1865* (New York & London: Garland Publishing, Inc., 1994), pp. 49–73. For further information on both Eckhard and Erben, see: *A History of the Lutheran Church in South Carolina* (Columbia: The South Carolina Synod of the Lutheran Church in America, 1971); and Leonard Ellinwood, *The History of American Church Music* (New York: Morehouse-Gorham Company, 1953).

26. See the article on "Prussian Union" in Lueker, *Lutheran Cyclopedia*, p. 860.

27. *Documentary History of the Pennsylvania Ministerium*, p. 469.

28. Ibid., 476.

29. *Das Gemeinschaftliche Gesangbuch, zum gottesdienstlichen Gebrauch der Lutherischen und Reformierten Gemeinden in Nord-America.* Auf Verlagen der meisten Prediger beyder Benennungen gesammelt, und von den Committeen zweyer Ministerien geprueft und genehmiget. (Zweite Auflage; Baltimore: Gedruckt und herausgegeben von Schaeffer und Maund, 1817).

30. Preface, III.

31. Ibid. While the Preface to this Common Hymnbook notes that "this book has the purpose of breaking down the wall of partition between Lutherans and Reformed," Claus Harms could proclaim, in his new "Ninety-five Theses" written for the 300th anniversary of the Lutheran Reformation as a rebuke, in part, to the unionism he saw in Germany: "To say that time has removed the wall of partition between Lutherans and Reformed, is not a straightforward mode of speech. It is necessary to ask which fell away from the faith of their Church, the Lutherans or the Reformed? or both?" [Thesis #77]

32. Reed, *The Lutheran Liturgy*, p. 171.

33. From the *Preface*.

34. From the *Preface* to *Das Gemeinschaftliche Gesangbuch*.

35. Quoted in Henkel, *History of the Tennessee Synod*, p. 6. Gottlieb Schober (1756–1838), was born in Bethlehem, Pennsylvania. Trained in the Moravian faith, he became a pastor in the North Carolina Synod. He helped form the General Synod in 1820. Within a decade Schober was to be a member of the committee which would produce the General Synod's first hymnbook, *Hymns, Selected and Original*, in 1828.

36. Ibid., p. 6.

37. *Neues Gemeinschaftliches Gesangbuch zum gottesdienstlichen Gebrauch der Lutherischen und Reformierten Gemeinden in Nord-Amerika*; mit einem Anhange enthaltend: eine Sammlung von etwa 150 Liedern und etlichen Gebeten (New York: Verlag von Wilhelm Radde, 1850).

38. Nicum, *Geschichte*, p. 194.

39. These "common hymnbooks" continued to be a problem among the Lutherans as late as the introduction of the General Council's *Kirchenbuch* in 1877. The problem was made more difficult of solution with the appearance of these books with altered title pages indicating they were "Evangelical Lutheran" books. See Nicum, *Geschichte*, p. 275.

40. For a fuller treatment of this controversy, see David A. Gustafson, *Lutherans in Crisis: The Question of Identity in the American Republic* (Minneapolis: Fortress Press, 1993).

41. Benson, *The English Hymn*, p. 416.

42. Ibid.

43. *Minutes of the Proceedings of the General Synod of the Evangelical Lutheran Church in the United States*; convened at Frederick, (Md.) October, 1825. (Frederick: Printed by Charles Nagle, 1825), p. 9.

44. *Minutes of the Proceedings of the General Synod of the Ev. Lutheran Church in the United States*. Convened at Gettysburg, Pa. October, 1827. (Gettysburg: Printed at the Press of the Theol. Seminary, H. C. Neinstedt, printer, 1827), p. 7.

45. *Hymns, selected and original, for public and private worship*. Published by the General Synod of the Ev. Lutheran Church. First edition. Gettysburg: Stereotyped by L. Johnson, Phila., 1828).

46. A later revised edition of 1868 includes three texts by S. S. Schmucker: nos. 456, 555, and 898.

47. Benson, *The English Hymn*, p. 417.

48. Ibid.

49. Ibid.

50. Ernest E. Ryden, "Hymnbooks," *The Encyclopedia of the Lutheran Church* (Minneapolis: Augsburg Publishing House, 1965), 1085.

51. Quoted from the *Preface* to the 1828 hymnbook in "The New Hymn Book," *The Evangelical Lutheran Intelligencer*, IV (September, 1829), 193.

52. Ibid., IV (September, 1829), 193.

53. Reed, *The Lutheran Liturgy*, p. 177.

54. *Proceedings of the Eighth Convention of the General Synod*. Convened at York, Penn., June, 1835, (Troy, N. Y.: N. Tuttle, printer, 1835), p. 15.

55. *Verhandlungen der Neunten General-Synode der Evangelisch-Lutherischen Kirche in den Vereinigten Staaten*. Gehalten zu Hagerstown, Md., May, 1837. (Gettysburg: Gedruckt bei Heinrich C. Heinstedt, 1837), p. 17.

56. *Evangelical Review*, XVI (April 1865), 204.

57. William Morton Reynolds (1812–1876) was born in Fayette County, Pennsylvania, and was a graduate of both Jefferson College at Canonsburg and the Gettysburg Theological Seminary. He was a professor at Pennsylvania College (associated with the seminary) from 1833–1850, except for 1835/36 when he served as pastor at Deerfield, New Jersey. In 1850 he became president of Capitol University, Columbus, Ohio, and subsequently held the same position at Illinois State University from 1857–1860. In 1864 he entered the ministry of the Protestant Episcopal Church. According to Jacobs who personally interviewed Reynolds in later years, his "sole motive in leaving the Church in which he had done distinguished and valuable service was that every door for employment was closed against him."

58. Liemohn, op. cit., p. 141.

59. *Proceedings of the Fourteenth Convention of the General Synod.* Convened in New York, May 13, 1848 (Baltimore: Printed at the Publication Rooms of the Evangelical Lutheran Church, 1848), pp. 33–40.

60. In the "Advertisement to the Enlarged Edition" it was noted that "the table of *German* hymns promised in the Preface to the former edition . . . is also herewith furnished. . . . It is hoped that this will not only facilitate the singing of these hymns, but also tend to improved our church music, by the introduction of a number of well-known and standard German tunes, with which a large body of our members are already familiar in the German."

61. No. 976 in the Revised Edition.

62. No. 977.

63. No. 916 in the Revised Edition.

64. *Book of Worship*. Published by the General Synod of the Lutheran Church in the United States (Philadelphia: Board of Publication, 1871)

65. Benson, *The English Hymn*, p. 418–419.

66. *Evangelical Review*, XVI (January, 1865), 28–29.

67. Ibid.

68. *Documentary History of the Pennsylvania Ministerium*, p. 542.

69. *Verhandlungen der Gen. Synode der Evangelisch-Lutherischen Kirche*

in der Vereinigten Staaten von Nord-Amerika (Gettysburg: Gedruckt in der Druckerey des Theol. Seminariums, 1827), p. 11.

70. Ibid. See also Nicum, *Geschichte*, p. 194n.

71. Ibid., pp. 194–195.

72. *Verhandlungen der Gen. Synode der Evangelisch-Lutherischen Kirche in der Vereinigten Staaten von Nord-Amerika (1833)*, op. cit., p. 15.

73 *Evangelische Liedersammlung, genommen aus der Lieder-sammlung und dem Gemeinschaftlichen Gesangbuch, zum bequemeren Gebrauch in den evangelischen Gemeinen* (Gettysburg: Steroetypirt von L. Johnson, 1837). This copy in my possession notes that the hymnbook was copyright in 1833.

74. Reed, *The Lutheran Liturgy*, p. 171.

Chapter 6: The Hymnody of the Scandinavian Immigrants
(pp. 111–120)

1. Carl F. Reuss, *Profiles of Lutherans in the U. S. A.* (Minneapolis: Augsburg Publishing House, 1982), p. 95, points out that about 58% of American Lutherans are of German ancestry, and about 28% of Scandinavian ancestry.

2. Much of the following material is based on the excellent summary found in Oscar N. Olson, *The Augustana Lutheran Church in America 1860–1910: The Formative Period* (Davenport, Iowa: Published under the auspices of the Executive Council of the Augustana Lutheran Church, 1956) and Joel W. Lundeen's article on Swedish Lutheran hymnody in *Hymnal Companion to the Lutheran Book of Worship*. Marilyn Stulken ed. (Philadelphia: Fortress Press, 1981). See also a brief treatment in Liemohm, *The Chorale*. Other sources containing helpful information include Clifford Ansgar Nelson, "Pulpit and Altar," (Rock Island: Augustana Press, 1960), p. 189ff.; and Evald B. Larson, "Music, Art, and Architecture in Our Church," *After Seventy-Five Years* (Rock Island: Augustana Book Concern, 1935), pp. 119–136.

3. Lundeen, "Swedish Hymnody," p. 47.

4. Perhaps best known for her text "Children of the heavenly Father."

5. Liemohn, *The Chorale*, pp. 143–144. This songbook was the first publication to come off the press which had been established in 1856 in Galesburg, Illinois, by T. N. Hasselquist, one of the early leaders among the Swedish Lutherans in America, and first president of the Augustana Synod. See Nelson, *Centennial Essays*, p. 190.

6. Hasselquist was a pastor in Sweden from 1839–1852 when he came to America and settled in Galesburg, Illinois. He was the founder and first president of the Augustana Synod (1860–70), president of Augustana College and Seminary (1863–91), and editor of the church paper *Augustana* (1855–91).

7. Other similar collections were published by Eric Norelius in Minnesota (*Salems Sanger*), and by Olof Olsson in Lindsborg, Kansas. See Nelson, *Centennial Essays*, p. 189ff.

8. Olson, *The Augustana Lutheran Church*, p. 73.

9. *Hymnal and Order of Service for Churches and Sunday Schools.* By Authority of the Evangelical Lutheran Augustana Synod in North America (Rock Island: Augustana Book Concern, 1899).

10. *Hymnal and Order of Service for Churches and Sunday Schools.* By Authority of the Evangelical Lutheran Augustana Synod of North America. With Music. (Rock Island: Lutheran Augustana Book Concern, 1901). The tunes were largely from the Synod's *Koralbok* and from Aug. Lagergren's *Svensk Koralbok* (after Haeffner). When a second setting is given it follows the rhythmic form of the melody and is taken from Schoeberlein's *Schatz des liturgischen Chor- und Gemeinde-gesangs* and from the books of Layriz, Brauer, Endlich, and similar volumes. The Preface notes that the use of the rhythmic form of the chorale melody is "earnestly advocated as best adapted to insure fresh and vigorous congregational singing."

11. *The Hymnal and Order of Service.* Authorized by the Evangelical Lutheran Augustana Synod (Rock Island, Ill.; Augustana Book Concern, 1925).

12. E. E. Ryden, twenty years later, would become the secretary of the committee which prepared the *Service Book and Hymnal* of 1958.

13. Mandus Egge, "Scandinavian Hymnody: Norwegian," *Hymnal Companion to the Lutheran Book of Worship*. Marilyn Kay Stulken, ed. (Philadelphia: Fortress Press, 1981), p. 37.

14. John M. Jensen, *The United Evangelical Lutheran Church: An*

Interpretation (Minneapolis: Augsburg Publishing House, 1964), p. vi.

15. Liemohn, *The Chorale*, p. 146.

16. Jensen, *The United Evangelical Lutheran Church: An Interpretation*, p. 152.

17. Ibid., p. 153.

18. See Enok Mortensen, *The Danish Lutheran Church in America* (Philadelphia: Board of Publication, Lutheran Church in America, 1967), p. 189.

19. Ibid., p. 164.

20. *Hymnal for Church and Home*. Published by the Danish Evangelical Lutheran Synods in America (Third Edition, Revised and Enlarged; Blair, Nebraska: Danish Lutheran Publishing House, 1938).

21. Liemohn, *The Chorale*, p. 145. See also Gerhard M. Cartford, "Music in the Norwegian Lutheran Church: A Study of Its Development and Its Transfer to America, 1825–1917" (Dissertation: University of Minnesota, 1961).

22. Ibid., p. 128. For additional information on Lindemann, see Gerhard M. Cartford, "The Contribution of Ludwig M. Lindemann to the Hymnology of the Norwegian Church" (Master's Thesis, Union Theological Seminary, 1950); also C. Howard Smith, *Scandinavian Hymnody from the Reformation to the Present* (Metuchen, NJ & London: The American Theological Library Association and the Scarecrow Press, Inc., 1987).

23. Ibid., p. 124.

24. O. M. Sandvik, *Norsk Koralhistorie* (Oslo: H. Aschehouh & Co., 1930). Quoted in Liemohn, *The Chorale*, p. 34.

25. *Hymnbook for the use of Evangelical Lutheran Schools and Congregations* (Decorah, Iowa: Lutheran Publishing House, 1879).

26. *Der Lutheraner*, XXXV (July 1, 1879), 104. See English translation of his comments in Carl Schalk, *The Roots of Hymnody in the Lutheran Church—Missouri Synod* (St. Louis: Concordia Publishing House, 1965), p. 39.

27. *Church and Sunday School Hymnal* (Minneapolis: Augsburg Publ.

House, 1898). Laurence N. Field mentions in passing two earlier endeavors without, however, naming them. He refers to an English hymnbook published in 1884 containing 130 hymns which "scandalously neglected our Norwegian heritage" and to a "modest Sunday School hymnbook, compiled by D. G. Ristad" in 1898. See Laurence N. Field, "Our Heritage of Music," *Norsemen Found a Church* (Minneapolis: Augsburg Publishing House, 1953), pp. 379–388.

28. *Christian Hymns for Church, School and Home* (Decorah: Lutheran Publishing House, 1898). This excellent little collection of 309 hymns and 12 doxologies was rich in Reformation hymnody and retained the rhythmic form of most of the chorales. Tunes and settings were largely from the work of Ludvig Lindemann, and from the Hoelter *Choralbuch*, Brauer's *Choralbuch*, and from the *Church Book* of the General Council.

29. Armas K. E. Holmio, "Suomi Synod," *The Encyclopedia of the Lutheran Church* (Minneapolis: Augsburg Publishing House, 1965), 1373, suggests that "More than half of the 900 colonists in 'New Sweden,' the Swedish settlement along the Delaware River, had been Finns."

Chapter 7: Movements toward a More Confessional Hymnody
(pp. 121–152)

1. Carl S. Meyer, ed. *Moving Frontiers: Readings in the History of the Lutheran Church—Missouri Synod* (St. Louis: Concordia Publishing House, 1964), p. 68.

2. Charles Burney, *The Present State of Music in Germany, the Netherlands, and United Provinces.* Facsimile of the 1775 London edition. 2 vols. (New York: Broude Brothers, 1969), II:279–281.

3. *Evang. Kirchenzeitung*,1847, No. 84. Quoted in Johann Daniel von der Heydt, *Geschichte der Evangelischen Kirchen-musik in Deutschland* (Berlin: Trowitzsch & Son, 1926), p. 195.

4. For a brief summary of these two immigrant groups see Wentz, op. cit., p. 114ff.

5. See Eugene W. Camann, "1839 Prussian Migration to Buffalo, N. Y. and Wisconsin," *Confessional Lutheran Migrations to America.* Published by the Eastern District of The Lutheran Church—Missouri Synod in observance of the 150 Anniversary of these Migrations of German Lutherans, 1988.

6. *Zweiter Synodal-Brief von der Synode der aus Preuszen ausgewanderten lutherischen Kirche*, versammelt zu Buffalo, N. Y. in July 1848 (Buffalo: Gedruckt bei Brunk u. Domedion, 1850), p. 5.

7. *Evangelisch-Lutherisches Kirchen-Gesang-Buch*, worin die gebraeuchlichsten alten Kirchen-Lieder Dr. M. Luther: und anderer reinen Lehrer und Zeugen Gottes, zu Befoerderung der wahren Gottseligkeit ohne Abaenderunger enthalten sind, fuer Gemeinen, welche sich zur unveraenderten Augsburgischer Confession bekennen (Buffalo: Gedruckt mit Georg Zahm's Schriften, 1842).

8. *Preface*, p. VI.

9. The complete listing of sources is given in the *Preface*, p. III.

10. The editions of 1559 were exact reprints of the edition of 1551 printed in Leipzig; the 1551 edition was an enlarged version of the original printing of 1545. See Johannes Zahn, *Die Melodien der deutschen evangelischen Kirchlieder* (Reprografischer Nachdruck der Ausgabe Guetersloh 1893; Hildes-heim: Georg Olms Verlagsbuchhandlung, 1963), VI, 32, 40, 43.

11. *Preface*, p. V.

12. Ibid., p. IV.

13. The *Vorwort* to the 1891 edition lists the following editions: second edition, 1848; third edition, 1858; fourth edition, 1864; fifth edition, 1879; sixth edition, 1885; seventh edition, 1891. The Preface to the fourth edition, however, is dated March 18, 1865. In another discrepancy the *Fuenfter Synodal-Brief* notes the appearance of the third edition in 1856.

14. "Etwas ueber das Kirchenlied," *Die Wachende Kirche*, XXXXIV (August 15, 1910), 124.

15. The story of the hymnody of the Saxon immigrants is told more completely in Carl Schalk, *The Roots of Hymnody in The Lutheran Church—Missouri Synod* (St. Louis: Concordia Publishing House, 1965). See also James Leonard Brauer, *The Hymnals of The Lutheran Church—Missouri Synod*. STM thesis, Concordia Seminary, St. Louis, 1967.

16. These included hymnbooks from Dresden, Marburg, Schleswig, Pommerania, Prussia, Hamburg, Bavaria, and Osnabrueck. See "Die Gesangbuecher," *Der Lutheraner*, VII (October 29, 1850), 35. Jon D. Vieker, "C. F. W. Walther: Editor of Missouri's First and Only German Hymnal,"

Concordia Historical Institute Quarterly, Vol. 65, No. 2 (Summer 1992) points out that the Dresden hymnbook was likely the predominant hymnbook used in the St. Louis congregation.

17. Minutes of Trinity Congregation, St. Louis, Missouri, November 10, 1845, transcript, Concordia Historical Institute. A summary of the congregational actions regarding this hymnbook may be found in O. A. Dorn, "Early Printing in the Missouri Synod," *Concordia Historical Institute Quarterly*, XXIV (April, 1951), 6.

18. *Kirchengesangbuch fuer Evangelisch-Lutherische Gemeinden unge-aenderter Augsburgischer Confession* darin des seligen D. Martin Luthers und anderes geistreichen Lehrer gebrauchlichste Kirchen-Lieder enthalten sind. (New York: Gedruckt fuer die Herausgeber bei H. Ludwig. Im Verlag der deutschen evang. luth. Gemeinde U. A. C. im St. Louis, Mo., 1847).

19. *Der Lutheraner*, III (February 9, 1847), 70.

20. Just who these pastors were is not clear. However, six laymen from Walther's congregation were selected to form the hymnbook committee at its January 1846 meeting: Friedric Barthel, Tschirpe, Hermann Wichmann, Carl Roschke, Rechmann, and Heinrich Abt. In appreciation for his labors on the hymnbook, Walther received from his congregation five cords of winter wood. See Brauer, *Hymnals of The Lutheran Church—Missouri Synod*, p. 25f.

21. "Lutherisches Kirchengesangbuch," *Der Lutheraner*, III (June 15, 1847), 84. Although the article is unsigned, it was apparently written by Walther himself.

22. See, for example, F.[riedrich] L.[ochner], "Ein Wort ueber Kirchenmelodien," *Der Lutheraner*, III (August 10, 1847), 139-40; [C. F. W. Walther] "Von alten und neuen Melodien," *Der Lutheraner*, VII (November 26, 1850), 52–55; G.[ustav] Sch[aller], "Was ist's mit den rhythmischen Choraelen?", *Der Lutheraner*, IX (May 10, 1853) 122–124; A. Hoyer, "Von rhythmischen Gesaenge in der christlichen Kirche," *Der Lutheraner*, X (July, 1854) 177–181.

23. Dorn, "Early Printing in the Missouri Synod," XXIV, 7–9.

24. Schalk, *The Roots of Hymnody*, passim.

25. Martin Guenther, *Dr. C. F. W. Walther* (St. Louis: Lutherischer Concordia-Verlag, 1890), p. 6.

26. In June 1867, for example, the Joint Synod of Ohio sought the cooperation of the Missouri Synod and the General Council for the publication of a new Lutheran hymn book in the German language. See P. A. Peter and Wm. Schmidt, *Geschickte der Allgemeinen Evang. Lutherischen Synode von Ohio und anderen Staaten* (Columbus: Verlagshandlung der Synode, 1900), p. 186.

27. *Concordanz zum Kirchen-Gesangbuch fuer ev.-luth. Gemeinden Ungeaenderter Augsburgischer Confession* (St. Louis: Lutherischer Concordia-Verlag, 1885).

28. "Concordanz zum Kirchengesangbuch," *Der Lutheraner*, XLI (March 15, 1885), 48.

29. *CXVII Geistliche Melodien meist aus dem 16. und 17. Jahr. in ihren urspruenglichen Rhythmen zweistimmig gesetzt* von Dr. Friedr. Layriz (Erlangen: Theodor Blaesing, 1839). Additional volumes followed in 1848, 1850, 1857, and 1862.

30. Minutes of Trinity Congregation, St. Louis, Mo., January 8, 1849, transcript, Concordia Historical Institute.

31. Friedrich Layriz, *Kern des deutschen Kirchengesangs*. 4 vols. (Noerdlingen: C. H. Beck'-sche Buchhandlung, 1844–55).

32. *Evangelisch-Lutherisches Choralbuch fuer Kirche und Haus*. Sammlung der gebraeuchlichsten Choraele der lutherischen Kirche ausgezogen und unveraendert abgedruckt aus "Kern des deutschen Kirchengesangs" von Dr. Fr. Layriz." (St. Louis: Verlag von L. Volkening, 1863).

33. H. F. Hoelter, ed. *Choralbuch*. Eine Sammlung der gangbarsten Choraele der evang.-lutherischen Kirche, meist Dr. Fr. Layriz nebst den wichtigsten Saetzen (St. Louis: Lutherischer Concordia Verlag, 1886).

34. *Mehrstimmiges Choralbuch* zu dem "Kirchengesangbuch fuer Evangelisch-Lutherische Gemeinden Ungeaenderter Augsburgischer Confession," ed. Karl Brauer (St. Louis, Mo.: Concordia Publishing House, 1888).

35. The story of why there should appear two so similar chorale books from the same publisher within two year is told in Schalk, *The Roots of Hymnody*, p. 35–38.

36. *Leiturgia*, I, 91.

37. *Agende fuer christliche Gemeinden des lutherischen Bekenntnisses.* Noerdlingen: C. H. Beck'schen Buchhandlung, 1844.

38. For a fuller description of the worship of the Bavarian communities, see Carl Schalk, "Sketches of Lutheran Worship," *Handbook of Church Music,* ed. Carl Halter and Carl Schalk. (St. Louis: Concordia Publishing House, 1978), p. 86–90.

39. See Lueker, *Lutheran Cyclopedia,* p. 519f.

40. Wilhelm Loehe, *Agende fuer christliche Gemeinden des lutherischen Bekenntnisses,* 2nd ed. (Noerdlingen: C. H. Beck'sche Buchhandlung, 1853). See also Layriz' *Liturgie eines vollstaen digen Hauptgottesdienstes nach lutherischem Typus.*

41. Geo. J. Fritschel, *Quellen und Dokumente zur Geschickte und Lehrstellung der ev.-luth. Synode von Iowa u. a. Staaten* (Chicago: Wartburg Publishing House, 1916), p. 139.

42. Johannes Deindoerfer, *Geschichte der Evangel.-Luth. Synode von Iowa und anderen Staaten* (Chicago: Verlag des Wartburg Publishing House, 1897), p. 105. The Raumer hymnbook was undoubtedly the *Sammlung geistlicher Lieder,* nebst einem Anhang von Gebeten. 2nd ed. (Stuttgart: S. G. Liesching, 1846) assembled by Karl von Raumer.

43. Ibid., p. 106.

44. Chiliasm, altar and pulpit fellowship, and secret societies.

45. Deindoerfer, op. cit., p. 183. See also "Das neue Gesang-buch des General Council," *Der Lutheraner,* XXXII (November 15, 1878), 171-172.

46. Nicum, *Geschickte,* p. 193. The Synod of West Pennsylvania was also involved in the preparation of this hymnbook. The signers of the Preface included for the Synod of Pennsylvania: J. Miller, C. R. Demme, G. A. Reichert, D. Ulrich, and J. Becker; for the Synod of New York: C. F. Stohlmann; for the Synod of West Pennsylvania: S. S. Schmucker, J. Albert, and A. G. Deininger. The Joint Synod of Ohio had also expressed an interest in the preparation of this book.

47. *Deutsches Gesangbuch fuer die Evangelisch-Lutherische Kirche in den Vereinigten Staaten.* Herausgegebnen mit Kirchlicher Genehmigung (Philadelphia: Druck und Verlag von L. A. Wollenweber, 1849).
This *Deutsches Gesangbuch* must be distinguished from a later book published exactly a decade later, *Deutsches Gesangbuch, Ein Auswahl*

geistlicher Lieder aus allen Zeiten der christlichen Kirche fuer oeffentlichen und haeuslichen Gebrauch (Philadelphia: Lindsay and Blakiston, 1859), prepared by Philip Schaff and subsequently adopted for use by the German Reformed Church.

In 1861, two years following the publication of Schaff's *Deutsches Gesangbuch*, G. F. Landenberger, a teacher at St. Michael and Zion Church in Philadelphia and organist at the St. Paul mission there, compiled a *Choral-Buch fuer die Orgel. Mit Zwischenspielen versehen, und fuer den vierstimmigen Vermaasen des deutschen Gesangbuches fuer Evangelisch-Lutherische Kirche in den Vereinigten Staaten, sowie zu denen des deutschen Gesangbuches fuer die Reformierte Kirche von Philipp Schaff, Dr. u. Prof. der Theologie* (Philadelphia: The Kohler Publishing Co., 1861). While not strictly speaking an official publication of the Pennsylvania Ministerium, it apparently had its blessing, as the Preface to the collection indicates.

48. Nicum, *Geschichte*, p. 195.

49. "Die Kirchengesangbuecher," *Der Lutheraner*, VII (October 1, 1850),pp. 20–21; VII, 27–28; VII, 35–37; VII, 42–44.

50. Ibid., VII, 20.

51. Ibid., VII, 20–21.

52. Ibid., VII, 28. For what is apparently Walther's reply to a letter from a reader of *Der Lutheraner* suggesting that the criticism of the "Pennsylvanische Gesangbuch" was perhaps due to a desire to contribute to the greater circulation of the Missouri Synod hymnbook, see "Das neue Pennsylvanische Gesangbuch, *Der Lutheraner*, VII, (Nov. 26, 1850), pp. 55-56.

53. "The New German Hymn Book," *The Evangelical Review*, I (April, 1850), 590–594. The review, signed "R." is apparently by William M. Reynolds, editor of this journal.

54. Ibid.

55. *Proceedings of the One Hundred and Third Annual Session of the German Evangelical Lutheran Ministerium of Pennsylvania and the Adjacent States* (Philadelphia: L. A. Wollenweber, 1850), p. 15.

56. Nicum, *Geschichte*, p. 195. This same Wilhelm Radde had published in 1849 the *Neues Gemeinschaftliche Gesangbuch, zum gottesdienstlicher Gebrauch der Lutherischen und Reformierten Gemeinden in*

Nord-Amerika mit einem Anhang, enthaltend: eine Sammlung von etwa 150 Liedern und etlichen Geben (New York: Verlag von Wilhelm Radde, 1849). The hymnbook to which Nicum refers as "Das neue gemeinschaftliche Gesangbuch" may be the 1850 edition of the above-mentioned hymnbook, but with Demme's "Deutsches Gesangbuch" incorporated into it as an appendix, as Nicum suggests.

57. *Proceedings of the One Hundred and Third Annual session of the German Evangelical Lutheran Ministerium of Pennsylvania and Adjacent States*, pp 15–16.

58. Nicum, *Geschichte*, p. 195.

59. *Deutsches Gesangbuch fuer die Evangelisch-Lutherische Kirche in den Vereinigten Staaten*. Herausgegeben mit kirchlicher Genehmigung. Neue vermehrte Ausgabe. (New York and Philadelphia: J. E. Stohlmann and John G. Maier, 1897), IV. The Preface is dated December 25, 1891. A second edition appeared in 1894. A printing of this second edition appeared as late as 1914.

60. See Lueker, *Lutheran Cyclopedia*, p. 757.

61. Peter and Schmidt, *Geschichte der Synode von Ohio*, p. 757. Ryden, "Hymnbook," *Encyclopedia of The Lutheran Church*, p. 1087, refers to a "German hymnal authorized by the Lutheran Conference of the Ministerium of Pennsylvania in western Pennsylvania, titled *Das neue Gesangbuch* which was published in 1816 and contained 139 hymns.

62. Peter and Schmidt, *Geschichte der Synode von Ohio*, p. 121.

63. Ibid., p. 169.

64. Ibid., p. 173.

65. Both Lehmann and Loy were conservative leaders, having led the Ohio Synod in 1898 to declare unconditional acceptance of the Lutheran Confessions. Both served terms as president of the Ohio Synod, Lehmann also serving several terms as president of the Synodical Conference.

66. Meyer, *Moving Frontiers*, p. 262.

67. Peter and Schmidt, *Geschichte der Synode von Ohio*, p. 186.

68. *Gesangbuch fuer Gemeinden des Evangelisch Lutherischen Bekennt-nisses*. Herausgegeben von der Allgemeinen Ev. Luth. Synode von Ohio u.

a. St. (Columbus, Ohio: Druck von Schulze und Gaszmann, 1870).

69. Benson, *The English Hymn*, p. 419.

70. *A Collection of Hymns and Prayers for Public and Private Worship.* Published by order of the Evangelical Lutheran Joint Synod of Ohio (Zanesville: printed at the Lutheran Standard office, 1845).

71. At the meeting of the Joint Synod of Ohio, April 22–29, 1853, the president, Pastor J. Wagenhals, refers to the important matter of an English hymnbook. See Peter and Schmidt, *Geschichte der Synode von Ohio*, p. 127.

72. *Collection of Hymns for Public and Private Worship.* Published by order of the Evangelical Lutheran Joint Synod of Ohio (Columbus: n.d.). As to the exact dating of this book, it is evident that it had not yet appeared in April, 1853. Benson lists the 2nd edition as published in 1855. The copy examined and in the possession of the library at Concordia Seminary, St. Louis is dated 1855, but contains no indication that it is a 2nd edition.

73. Benson, *The English Hymn*, p. 420.

74. From the *Preface.*

75. Ibid.

76. The *Preface* to this book interesting notes that "the additional figures, at the head of each hymn, designate the metre according to a new plan, introduced in the "Cantica Sacra," a new music-book, which, it is expected, will be introduced in many of our congregations." The *Cantica Sacra; A Collection of Church Music, Embracing, Besides Some New Pieces, A Choice Selection of German and English Chorals, Set Pieces, Chants, Etc., from the Best European and American Authors; Adapted to the Various Meters in Use; With the text in German and English,* by J. J. Fast, Ev. Luth. Minister, Canton, Ohio (Hudson, Ohio: Hudson Book Company, 1854), was a shaped note collection of four-part settings of hymns and chorales, over half of them based on Layriz, which utilized the rhythmic form of the chorale melodies. See *Der Lutheraner*, XII (January 15, 1856), 88. This collection by Pastor J. J. Fast of Canton, Ohio, was also promoted to a degree in the Missouri Synod, being sold through Otto Ernst in St. Louis.

77. Peter and Schmidt, *Geschichte der Synode von Ohio*, p. 187. This was the same meeting at which the Joint Synod of Ohio sought, unsuccessfully, to seek the cooperation of the Missouri Synod and the General Council in producing a common German hymnbook.

78. *Evangelical Lutheran Hymnal.* Published by Order of the Ev. Lutheran Joint Synod of Ohio and Other States (Columbus, Ohio: Ohio Synodical Printing House, 1880). This hymnbook indicates that there is a "book of tunes shortly to be published by order of the Joint Synod."

79. *Evangelical Lutheran Hymnal.* Published by order of the First English District of the Joint Synod of Ohio and Other States (Columbus: Lutheran Book Concern, 1908).

80. Reed, *The Lutheran Liturgy,* p. 177.

81. For a summary of the development of the General Council's *Church Book* and the crucial role played by the Pennsylvania Ministerium in its formation, together with a detailed listing of the changing personnel of the Church Book Committee, see S. E. Ochsenford, *Documentary History of the General Council of the Evangelical Lutheran Church in North America* (Philadelphia: General Council Publication House, 1912), pp. 412–426. Hereafter referred to as the *Documentary History of the General Council.*

82. Ibid., p. 415.

83. For brief biographical sketches of these two men, see Reed, *The Lutheran Liturgy,* pp. 180, 190.

84. *Hymns for the use of the Evangelical Lutheran Church.* By authority of the Ministerium of Pennsylvania (Philadelphia: J. B. Rogers, 1865). According to Jacobs, the Rev. Frederick Bird was the editor with Dr. B. M. Schmucker as his adviser. See Henry E. Jacobs, "What Is a Real Lutheran Hymn," *Lutheran Church Review,* XLI (July, 1922), 210–219.

85. *Evangelical Review,* XVIII (January, 1866), 154.

86. Quoted in *Documentary History of the General Council,* p. 416.

87. *Evangelical Review,* XVII (April, 1866), 215.

88. Ibid.

89. Ibid., p. 211.

90. Ibid., p. 216.

91. Ibid., p. 218.

92. Ibid.

93. *Documentary History of the General Council*, p. 416.

94. Ibid.

95. Ibid., p. 417–418.

96. *Church Book For the Use of Evangelical Lutheran Congregations.* By authority of the General Council of the Evangelical Lutheran Church in America (Philadelphia: Lutheran Book Store, 1868).

97. *Documentary History of the General Council*, p. 229.

98. Harriet Reynolds Krauth Spaeth (1845–1925) was born in Baltimore, Maryland, on September 21, 1845. She was married in 1880 to Adolph Spaeth and had five children, perhaps the most famous being Sigmund Spaeth, noted American writer on music. Her father was Charles Porterfield Krauth and her grandfather Charles Philip Krauth, president of Gettysburg Theological Seminary.

99. Ibid., p. 282.

100. Reed, *The Lutheran Liturgy*, p. 179.

101. Benson, *The English Hymn*, p. 560–561.

102. *Hymns ancient and modern* for use in the services of the Church: with accompanying tunes compiled and arranged by William Henry Monk (London: Novello and Co., 1861).

103. Reed, *The Lutheran Liturgy*, p. 180.

104. *Evangelical Review*, XVI (July, 1865), 342.

105. Reed, *The Lutheran Liturgy*, p. 181.

106. Benson, *The English Hymn*, p. 562.

107. *Documentary History of the General Council*, p. 152f.

108. Nicum, *Geschickte*, p. 195. Fritschel was from the Iowa Synod as was G. M. Grossmann, President of the Iowa Synod from 1854–93, another member of the committee who Nicum omits from his list.

109. *Documentary History of the General Council*, p. 426.

110. Ibid., p. 232.

111. Ibid., p. 249.

112. *Choralbuch mit Liturgie und Chorgesaengen zum Kirchenbuch der Allgemeinen Kirchenversammlung*, Bearbeitet von J. Endlich (Philadelphia: United Lutheran Publication House, 1879.

113. *Documentary History of the General Council*, p. 428.

114. Ibid., p. 429.

115. Preface to Endlich's *Choralbuch*, p. Iff.

116. Ibid.

117. Nicum, *Geschichte*, p. 275.

118. Ibid., p. 196.

119. *Hymnbook for the use of Evangelical Lutheran Schools and Congregations* (Decorah: Lutheran Publishing House, 1879). The translator and editor of this hymnbook was Prof. August Crull of Concordia College, Ft. Wayne, Indiana.

120. See *Der Lutheraner*, XXXV (July 1, 1879), 104.

121. *Lutheran Hymns. For the Use of English Lutheran Missions* (St. Louis, Mo., 1882).

122. *Hymns of the Evangelical Lutheran Church. For the Use of English Lutheran Missions* (St. Louis: Concordia Publishing House, 1886).

123. *Hymns for Evangelical Lutheran Missions* (St. Louis: Concordia Publishing House, 1905).

124. In 1888 Concordia Publishing House was negotiating with Crull for the manuscript of an English hymnbook. Crull seems to have thought the Publishing House was taking too long to make up its mind in the matter and donated the manuscript to the English Lutheran Conference of Missouri and Other States. See the *Concordia Publishing House Commentator*, September, 1964, p. 5.

125. *Evangelical Lutheran Hymn Book*. Published by Order of the General

English Lutheran Conference of Missouri and Other States (Baltimore: Harry Lang, printer, 1889).

126. See W. G. Polack, *The Handbook to the Lutheran Hymnal.* 3rd rev. ed. (St. Louis: Concordia Publishing House, 1958), p. vi. In 1897 this committee included the Revs. Wm. Dallmann, C. C. Morhart, H. B. Hemmeter, Oscar Kaiser, Adam Detzer, and W. P. Sachs.

127. *Evangelical Lutheran Hymn-Book with Tunes* (St. Louis: Concordia Publishing House, 1912). Strictly speaking this was not simply a music edition of the 1889 or 1892 hymnal, as its enlarged size and reorganization of the arrangement of the hymns clearly indicates.

128. Ludwig Herman Ilse (1845–1931) was born in Hanover, Germany. Educated at Concordia Teachers College, Addison, Illinois, he served as teacher and organist successively at Pittsburgh, Pennsylvania (First Trinity), Chicago, Illinois (Zion), Brooklyn, New York (St. John's and, later, Trinity), and in Bedford, Ohio (Zion), as organist. His publications include: *Chorbuch* (with Wm Burhenn); *Taschenchorbuch* (with Burhenn); *Zwischenspiel*; *Saengerfreund*; *Kantional fuer Maennerchor*; *Choralbuch* (with H. Hoelter).

129. See Polack, op. cit., p. 526.

Chapter 8: Movements toward Consensus and Consolidation
(pp. 153–181)

1. The United Norwegian Lutheran Church was formed in 1890 as the result of a merger by the Norwegian Augustana Synod, the Norwegian Danish Conference, and the Anti-Missourians. The United Norwegian Lutheran Church was generally considered to be theologically in the middle between the other synods working on this hymnal. It was the largest of the three groups in 1898 with 1059 congregations with 123,000 communicant members.

2. The Norwegian Lutheran Church was formed in 1853. It was the bulwark of conservatism among Norwegian Lutherans in America. In 1898 it included 735 congregations with 66,000 communicant members.

3. The Hauge's Lutheran Synod exemplified Lutheran Pietism among the Norwegians and sprang from the teachings of layman Hans N. Hauge (1771–1824). Low-church Haugean immigrants were led in America by layman Elling Eielsen (1804–1883). The Hauge's Lutheran Synod itself was formed in 1875–76. By 1898 there were 217 congregations with approximately 17,500 communicant members.

4. John Dahle (b. 1853) was the leading hymnologist of the Norwegian Lutheran Church of America. He attended several Norwegian Lutheran colleges and seminaries in Minnesota, organized the Choral Union of the Norwegian Synod, and edited many choir books and wrote choral music. See also John Dahle, *Library of Christian Hymns*. tr. M. Caspar Johnshoy (Minneapolis: Augsburg Publishing House, 1924). 3 vols. This is essentially a handbook to *The Lutheran Hymnary*.

5. F. Melius Christiansen (1871–1955) emigrated to the United States in 1888. He studied at Augsburg College, Northwestern Conservatory of Music in Minneapolis, and the Royal Conservatory of Music in Leipzig. He was head of the music department at St. Olaf College from 1903–1943, where he organized the famed St. Olaf Lutheran Choir in 1912.

6. *Preface*.

7. We see here a thread which was to be common to many of the particular examples of the movement toward consolidation in the 20th century: the simultaneous efforts of work on a joint hymnbook, and discussions leading to closer cooperation and possible merger between various Lutheran groups. In some instances discussions toward closer cooperation came first; in other instances, work on a common hymnal came first. Regardless, both elements are frequently found together as various Lutheran church bodies found such joint work to be not only convenient, helpful, and necessary, but, in some cases, demanded by their particular understanding of scripture and the Lutheran Confessions.

8. *Christian Hymns for Church, School and Home* (Decorah: Lutheran Publishing House, 1898). This excellent collection of 309 hymns and 12 doxologies was rich in Reformation hymnody and retained the rhythmic form of the melody for most of the chorales. Tunes and settings were taken largely from the work of Ludvig Lindemann and from Hoelter's *Choralbuch*, Brauer's *Mehrstimmiges Choralbuch*, and from the *Church Book of the General Council*.

9. *Church and Sunday School Hymnal* (Minneapolis: Augsburg Publ. House, 1898).

10. *The Lutheran Hymnary* (Minneapolis: Augsburg Publishing House, 1913).

11. *Preface*, p. 3

12. Ibid.

13. Ibid.

14. Ibid. The following seven chorales appear in both the rhythmic and isometric forms: *Allein Gott in der Hoeh, Es ist gewisslich, Freu dich sehr, Herzlich tut mich, O Welt, ich muss dich lassen, Kommt her zu mir,* and *Wer nur den lieben Gott.* Of the chorales melodies included in this hymnbook, most are found in the isometric form.

15. Ibid. In this feature, unusual for the time, the hymns for the church year are arranged not only generally by season, but by Sunday or Festival in the season. Thus one or more hymns have been chosen for every Sunday in the church year.

16. *Concordia.* A Collection of Hymns and Spiritual Songs. (Minneapolis: Augsburg Publishing House, 1916).

17. Prepared by Revs. Andr. Bersagel, V. E. Boe, and S. O. Sigmond, the collection contained "those ever-living, ever-lasting, ever-spiritual chorals that come from Latin, German, and Scandinavian sources," "the most valuable hymns from the English-speaking world," and "the choicest Gospel hymns."

18. Ryden, "Hymnbook," *Encyclopedia of the Lutheran Church*, vol. II, p. 1089. Interesting is the inclusion in *Concordia* of a section of Temperance Hymns.

19. For a description of the development of the Common Service, see Reed, *The Lutheran Liturgy*, pp. 182–199. Soon after its adoption by the three original general bodies which joined in its preparation, it was in use by the Iowa Synod, the Joint Synod of Ohio, the Norwegian synods, the Missouri Synod, and later by the Augustana and Icelandic synods.

20. Ibid., p. 193.

21. The United Synod of the South was formed largely because of the division brought about by the Civil War. In 1867 it published its *Book of Worship* containing 465 hymns which were characterized by Benson as containing "little or nothing to distinguish them from the hymn books of the surrounding Evangelical denominations." [Benson, *The English Hymn*, p. 561].

22. Reed, *The Lutheran Liturgy*, p. 194.

23. Ibid.

24. Minutes of the General Council, 1897, p. 129.

25. Minutes of the General Council, 1901, p. 145. The volume referred to was the *Proof Copy of a Proposed New Hymnal* containing 541 hymns and prepared in 1899 by Dr. J. A. Seiss and published at his own expense. See Reed, op. cit., p. 199.

26. Minutes of the General Council, 1903, p. 157.

27. Minutes of the General Council, 1907, p. 243.

28. Ibid.

29. Minutes of the General Council, 1909, p. 100.

30. The position and influence of Luther D. Reed, who served as chairman of the General Council's Church Book Committee, Chairman of the Editorial Committee, Secretary of the Joint Committee and all five of its subcommittees, cannot be overestimated in assessing both the strengths and the weaknesses of this joint endeavor.

31. Minutes of the General Council, 1911, p. 223.

32. Ibid.

33. *Common Service Book and Hymnal* (Philadelphia: The Board of Publication of the United Lutheran Church in America, 1917).

34. Jeremiah Franklin Ohl (1850–1941) was an American Lutheran pastor, hymnist, liturgist, and editor who was active in deaconess and prison reform work. He graduated from the Lutheran Theological Seminary in Philadelphia and served as pastor in Pennsylvania from 1874–1893. He organized and directed the Lutheran Deaconess Motherhouse, Milwaukee, Wisconsin from 1893–1898. He served as chairman of the music sub-committee for the *Common Service Book and Hymnal*, arranged the first setting of the service, and generally supervised the music for the book. An article by Ohl, "The Liturgical Deterioration of the Seventeenth and Eighteenth Centuries," appeared in the *Memoirs of the Lutheran Liturgical Association*, IV,75–77. Nine original tunes of Ohl's are included in the *Common Service Book and Hymnal*.

35. Minutes of the General Council, 1911, p. 233.

36. See the *Preface* to the *Common Service Book and Hymnal*, p. 309.

37. See Henry E. Jacobs, "What Is a Real Lutheran Hymn," *Lutheran Church Review*, XLI (July 1922, 210–219. This article was written to meet the objection that the hymnal of the Common Service Book contained too small a proportion of hymns by Lutheran authors. Reed notes that this objection was voiced primarily in the Midwest. Reed, *The Lutheran Liturgy*, p. 201.

38. The one exception to the use of translations from the German was the work of Catherine Winkworth from whose work over fifty examples were included. Most all of Winkworth's translations which were selected, however, were from the later periods of German hymnody.

39. Jacobs, "What Is a Real Lutheran Hymn," *Lutheran Church Review*, XLI (July 1922), 215.

40. *American Lutheran Survey* (October 23, 1918). This quotation is contained in a review of the *Wartburg Hymnal* of 1918.

41. *The Wartburg Hymnal* was edited by O. Harding in response to requests from congregations beginning to hold English services in increasing numbers.

42. *American Lutheran Hymnal.* Compiled and edited by an Intersynodical Committee (Columbus, Ohio: The Lutheran Book Concern, 1930).

43. The Iowa Synod, organized in 1854, originally had ties with the Missouri Synod through the pastors that Wilhelm Loehe sent to Michigan and then to Iowa. These ties were broken because of doctrinal disagreements, thus giving cause for the formation of the Iowa Synod. In 1920 the Iowa Synod invited the Joint Synod of Ohio, which had for a time (1872–82) been a member of the Synodical Conference, for discussions on church union. Since 1918, the Iowa and Ohio Synods had altar and pulpit fellowship.

44. *Preface*, p. 3.

45. *Preface*.

46. Liturgically, the *American Lutheran Hymnal* included the Common Service and the Ohio Synod Order of Service together with Scripture Lessons, Introits, Collects and Gradual, the Passion History, and a table of Psalms.

47. For a brief description of the history of the Synodical Conference, see Lueker, *Lutheran Cyclopedia*, pp. 1030–32.

48. The English Synod of Missouri (1888), the Michigan Synod (1892), the Nebraska District Synod (1906), the Slovak Ev. Lutheran Church (1908), and the Norwegian Synod of the American Evangelical Lutheran Church (1920).

49. *Verhandlungen der zweiten Versammlung der Evang.-Luth. Synodal-Conferenz von Nord-Amerika*, zu Ft. Wayne, Ind., vom 16. bis zum 22 Juli 1873 (Columbus, Ohio: Druck von John J. Gaszmann, 1873), pp. 13–14.

50. *Verhandlungen der sechsten Versammlung der evange-lish-Lutherischen Synodal-Conferenz von Nord-Amerika*, zu Ft. Wayne, Ind., vom 18, bis 24 Juli 1877 (St. Louis, Mo.: Druckerie der Synode von Missouri, Ohio und anderen Staaten, 1877), p. 23ff.

51. C. R. Demme's *Deutsches Gesangbuch* of 1849.

52. The *Gemeinschaftliche Gesangbuecher.*

53. *Verhandlungen der zweiten Versammlung der Evang.-Luth. Synodal-Conferenz von Nord-Amerika*, p. 26–27.

54. Prior to this time the Norwegian Synod of the American Evangelical Lutheran Church had been using the *Lutheran Hymnary* of 1913; the Joint Synod of Wisconsin, Minnesota, Michigan and Other States had used the *Church Hymnal* which it published in 1910 and, since 1920, its *Book of Hymns*; the Slovak Evangelical Lutheran Synod had been using the *Evangelical Lutheran Hymn-Book* of 1912.

55. A summary of the action of the Missouri Synod in this regard is given in Polack, *Handbook to The Lutheran Hymnal*, vi–viii.

56. Bernard Schumacher is usually thought to have been responsible for the musical settings in *The Lutheran Hymnal*. Other members of the committee in the course of its work included: L. Fuerbringer, O. Kaiser, L. Blankenbuehler, J. Meyer, O. Hagedorn, N. A. Madsen, C. Anderson, J. Pelikan, Wm. Moll, A. Zich, A. Voss, A. Harstad, O. H. Schmidt, J. Bajus, J. Kucharik, and W. J. Schaefer.

Other individuals who assisted as members of subcommittees include: Revs. Wm. M. Czamanske, W. Lochner, W. Burhop, K. Ehlers, J. H. Deckmann, C. M. Waller, C. Hoffmann, C. Bergen, G. W. Fischer; the Rev. Profs. W. Schaller, W. Buszin, R. W. Heintze, M. Lochner; Profs. K. Haase, E. Becker; the Rev. Drs. J. H. Ott, P. E. Kretzmann, A. W. Wismar, and S. C. Ylvisaker.

57. Polack, *Handbook to The Lutheran Hymnal*, p. VII.

58. Reports appeared in the *Lutheran Witness* as follows: January 16, 1934; March 27, 1934; November 5, 1935; October 26, 1936; and November 9, 1937; a report in pamphlet form in the Spring of 1938; a report to the respective synods in 1938; a final comprehensive report in pamphlet form dated May 1, 1939.

59. *The Lutheran Hymnal*. Authorized by the Synods Constituting The Evangelical Lutheran Synodical Conference of North America (St. Louis: Concordia Publishing House, 1941).

60. Polack, *Handbook to The Lutheran Hymnal*, XI.

61. See the *Introduction* to the Common Hymnal, p. 285.

62. Ibid.

63. Letter from Dr. John Behnken, president of The Lutheran Church—Missouri Synod, to Dr. Luther D. Reed, quoted in Reed, *The Lutheran Liturgy*, p. 208. While it is true that the Missouri Synod had just published *The Lutheran Hymnal* in 1941, it is also true that the Missouri Synod had been most critical of the hymnal ventures of a number of the participants in this new project, and had shown, in general, a reluctance to become involved in any joint efforts with other Lutherans.

64. Reed, *The Lutheran Liturgy*, p. 217.

65. *Introduction* to the Common Hymnal, p. 286.

66. *Service Book and Hymnal of the Lutheran Church in America*. Authorized by the Churches cooperating in The Commission on the Liturgy and the Commission on the Hymnal, 1958. The book was jointly published by Augsburg Publishing House, Minneapolis, Minnesota; Augustana Book Concern, Rock Island, Illinois; Lutheran Publishing House, Blair, Nebraska; Finnish Lutheran Book Concern, Hancock, Michigan; United Lutheran Publication House, Philadelphia, Pennsylvania; and Wartburg Press, Columbus, Ohio.

67. Mortensen, *The Danish Lutheran Church*, p. 265. The *Hymnal for Church and Home* with 454 hymns contained about 150 Danish hymns; the *Service Book and Hymnal* with 602 hymns, by contrast, contained only seventeen Danish hymns.

68. Any brief perusal of the hymns of the early Lutheran Church of the 16th century cannot fail to reveal their didactic or teaching function. Thus Ulrich Leupold can say: "Luther's hymns were meant not to create a mood, but to

convey a message. They were a confession of faith, not of personal feelings. That is why, in the manner of folk songs, they present their subject vividly and dramatically, but without the benefit of ornate language and other poetic refinements. They were written not to be read but to be sung by a whole congregation." LW 53:197.

69. *Introduction* to the Common Hymnal, p. 286.

70. Herbert Lindemann was Chairman of the Committee on Liturgical Texts; Jaroslav Vajda was chairman of the Committee on Hymn Texts; and Paul Bunjes was chairman of both the Committee on Liturgical Music and the Committee on Music for the Hymns. Walter E. Buszin was to be editor of the revised hymnal, and Herbert Lindemann was presiding chairman of the Commission.

71. Fred L. Precht, "Worship Resources in Missouri Synod's History," *Lutheran Worship: History and Practice* (St. Louis: Concordia Publishing House, 1993), p. 106, notes that "little did the Commission on Worship envision the strong feelings of the Synod in support of a common hymnal for all Lutherans in America, a fact attested by the 16 (plus four unpublished) resolutions from congregations as well as pastoral conferences and districts favoring such a hymnal . . ."

72. *Proceedings*, 1965, p. 186.

73. The presentations at this meeting together with the resolutions adopted are contained in *Liturgical Reconnaissance*, ed. Edgar S. Brown, Jr. (Philadelphia: Fortress Press, 1968).

74. The ILCW consisted of eight members from the Lutheran Church in America; seven from the American Lutheran Church; seven from The Lutheran Church--Missouri Synod; and one each from the Synod of Evangelical Lutheran Churches (Slovak Synod) and the Evangelical Lutheran Church of Canada. The work of the Commission was delegated to four standing committees: a Committee on Liturgical Texts, Liturgical Music, Hymn Texts, and Hymn Music.

75. *Worship Supplement.* Authorized by the Commission on Worship, The Lutheran Church—Missouri Synod and Synod of Evangelical Lutheran Churches (St. Louis: Concordia Publishing House, 1969). It contained 93 hymns together with liturgical material, and was published in a tune-text edition and an edition for the organist.

76. *Lutheran Book of Worship.* Prepared by the churches participating in the Inter-Lutheran Commission on Worship: Lutheran Church in America,

The American Lutheran Church, The Evangelical Lutheran Church of Canada, The Lutheran Church—Missouri Synod. (Minneapolis and Philadelphia: Augsburg Publishing House and Board of Publication, Lutheran Church in America).

77. The modifications the committee felt necessary were contained in the *Report and Recommendations of the Special Hymnal Review Committee* (The Lutheran Church—Missouri Synod, 500 North Broadway, St. Louis, Missouri, May, 1978).

78. Robert Sauer, "Lutheran Worship (1982): The Special Hymnal Review Committee," *Lutheran Worship: History and Practice.* ed. Fred L. Precht. (St. Louis: Concordia Publishing House, 1993), p. 199. Sauer, a vice-president of the synod, was the chairman of the "Special Hymnal Review Committee."

79. *Lutheran Worship.* Prepared by the Commission on Worship of The Lutheran Church—Missouri Synod. (St. Louis: Concordia Publishing House, 1982).

80. Marilyn Kay Stulken, *Hymnal Companion to the Lutheran Book of Worship* (Philadelphia: Fortress Press, 1981), and Fred L. Precht, *Lutheran Worship: Hymnal Companion* (St. Louis: Concordia Publishing House, 1992).

81. *The Lutheran Witness*, June 1983, p. 30. Ethnocentrism, "politics," and other factors may have influenced the discussion of the two hymnals, but the Missouri Synod was more concerned about a "doctrinal reorientation" that seemed to pervade the LBW, often the result of omissions, for example, removing well-known hymns—especially deleting specific stanzas or changing phrases—that emphasized the redemption. For details, see *Convention Workbooks, the 52nd Regular Convention*, The Lutheran Church—Missouri Synod, July 1977, pp. 39–40; and *the 53rd Regular Convention*, July 1979, pp. 88–90; also the detailed study by Committee 1 of the Commission on Theology and Church Relations relative to the issue.

82. The history of the hymnals of the Wisconsin Synod is summarized briefly in Arnold O. Lehmann, "The WELS and its Hymnals," *Northwestern Lutheran*, June 1993, p. 198–199, and at greater length in James Cameron Grasby, *A Historical Survey and Brief Examination of the Hymnbooks Used Within the Wisconsin Evangelical Lutheran Synod*. MCM thesis, Concordia University, 1981.

83. For example, the *Gesangbuch fuer die Evangelisch-Lutherische Sct. Johannes-Kirche in Jefferson, Wisc.* which came into use in 1851. See Grasby, *Historical Survey*, p. 19.

84. In 1865 President Streissguth of the Wisconsin Synod appointed a committee to contact the Pennsylvania, New York, and Ohio Synods about the possibility of revising the old Pennsylvania hymnbook to make it more desirable for use by orthodox Lutherans. If unsuccessful, the committee was to consider compiling its own hymnal.

85. *Continuing in His Word* (Milwaukee: Northwestern Publishing House, 1951), p. 261.

86. For example, two hymns—"Eine Heerde und ein Hirt" and "Ihr Kinder des Hoechsten wie steht's um die Liebe"—were cited as undesirable to be included in an orthodox hymnbook. See Grasby, *Historical Survey.*

87. Arnold O. Lehmann, "The WELS and its Hymnals," *Northwestern Lutheran* (June 1993), 198–199, notes that no copy of the 1870 book is known to exist today.

88. Arnold Lehmann gives the date as "around 1905." Grasby suggests it may have been "printed first in 1911."

89. See H. Koller Moussa, "Addenda to the Book of Hymns," *Northwestern Lutheran,* August 18, 1926, p. 252.

90. Observers at this meeting from the Wisconsin Evangelical Lutheran Synod were Martin Albrecht and Kurt J. Eggert.

91. *Christian Worship: A Lutheran Hymnal.* Authorized by the Wisconsin Evangelical Lutheran Synod (Milwaukee, Wisconsin: Northwestern Publishing House, 1993).

92. *Christian Worship: Manual.* Gary Baumler and Kermit Moldenhauer, eds. (Milwaukee: Northwestern Publishing House, 1993). Authorized by the Commission on Worship of the Wisconsin Evangelical Lutheran Synod.

Appendix A

Occurrence of Selected Hymns
from the
Babst Hymnal (1545)
in
American Lutheran Hymnals

Hymnals

Hymnal	Year
Babst Gesangbuch	1545
Freylinghausen's Geistreiches Gesangbuch	1741
Psalmodia Germanica	1756
Muhlenberg's Erbauliche Liedersammlung	1786
Kunze's A Hymn and Prayer Book	1795
Henkel's Das Neu Eingerichtete Gesangbuch	1810
Quitman's Collection of Hymns	1814
Henkel's Church Hymn Book	1816
Das Geimeinschaftliche Gesangbuch	1817
Hymns, selected and original	1828
Evangelische Liedersammlung	1833
Grabau's Kirchensammlung	1842
Walther's Kirchengesangbuch	1847
Deutsches Gesangbuch	1849
Ohio Synod's Collection of Hymns	1855
General Council's Church Book	1868
Ohio Synod's Gesangbuch	1870
General Council's Kirchenbuch	1877
General Council's Kirchenbuch	1880
Ohio Synod's Ev. Luth. Hymnal	1880
Hymnal and Order of Service	1899
Ev. Luth. Hymn-Book	1912
The Lutheran Hymnary	1913
Common Service Book	1917
Hymnal for Church and Home	1927
The American Lutheran Hymnal	1930
The Lutheran Hymnal	1941
Service Book and Hymnal	1958
Lutheran Book of Worship	1978
Lutheran Worship	1982
Christian Worship: A Lutheran Hymnal	1993

Selected Hymn Texts from----
The Babst Hymnbook

Selected hymn texts (rows of the occurrence matrix):

- Ach Gott vom Himmel sieh darein
- All' Ehr' und Lob
- Aus tiefer Not
- Christ, der du bist Tag und Licht
- Christ fuhr gen Himmel
- Christ ist erstanden
- Christ lag in Todesbanden
- Christum wir sollen loben schon
- Christ unser Herr zum Jordan kam
- Der du bist drei in Einigkeit
- Der Tag der ist so freudenreich
- Durch Adams Fall
- Dies sind die heiligen zehn Gebot
- Ein feste Burg ist unser Gott
- Erhalt uns, Herr, bei deinem Wort
- Es ist das heil uns kommen her
- Es woll' uns Gott genaedig sein
- Es spricht der unweisen Mund
- Gelobet seist du, Jesu Christ
- Gott der Vater wohn' uns bei
- Gott sei gelobet
- Herr Christ der einige Gottes Sohn
- Herr Gott dich loben wir
- Jesaia, dem Propheten das geschah
- Jesus Christus, unser Heiland
- Komm, Gott Schoepfer, Heiliger Geist
- Komm, Heiliger Geist
- Mensch willst du leben seliglich
- Mit Fried' und Freud' ich fahr dahin
- Mitten wir im Leben sind
- Nun bitten wir den Heiligen Geist
- Nun freut euch lieben Christen gemein
- Nun laszt uns den Leib begraben
- Nun komm, der Heiden Heiland
- O Herre Gott, dein goettlich Wort
- Vater unser im Himmelreich
- Verleih uns Frieden gnaedichlich
- Vom Himmel hoch, da kom ich her
- Vom Himmel kam der Engel schar
- Was fuerchst du, Feind Herodias
- Waer' Gott nicht mit uns diese Zeit
- Wo Gott zum Haus
- Wohl dem, der in Gottesfurcht steht
- Wir glauben all' an einen Gott

Appendix B

Geistreiches Gesangbuch (1741)

Contents

Of the coming of Christ in the Flesh, or Advent Hymns
Of the coming of Christ for Judgment
Of the Incarnation and Birth of Christ
New Year's Hymns
About Jesus, His Names and Offices
On the Festival of the Transfiguration of Christ
On the Festival of the Purification of Mary
On the Festival of the Annunciation to Mary
Of the Suffering and Death of Jesus Christ
Of the Burial of Jesus Christ
Of the Ascension of Jesus Christ
Of the Holy Spirit and His Works, or Pentecost Hymns
Of God's Being and Attributes, or the Festival of the Holy Trinity
On the Festival of John the Baptist
On the Festival of the Visitation of Mary
On the Holy Angels, or the Festival of St. Michael

Of the Kindness of God and Christ
Of the Act of Creation, and Therefore the Evidence of God's Love and Glory
Of Godly Providence and Government
Of Sacred Scriptures
Of Holy Baptism
Of Holy Communion
Of True and False Christendom
Of Human Misery and Corruption
Of True Confession and Contrition
Of True Faith
Of the Christian Life and Conduct
Of Prayer
Of Spiritual Vigilance
Of Spiritual Struggle and Victory
Of Chastity
Of the Denial of One's Self and the World
Of the Desire for God and Christ
Of Love for Jesus
Of Brotherly and Common Love
Of the Imitation of Christ
Of the Mystery of the Cross
Of Christian Resignation
Of Patience and Perseverance
Of the Surrender of the Heart to God
Of Godly Peace
Of Joy in the Holy Spirit
Of the Joyfulness of Faith
Of the Praise of God

Erbauliche Liedersammlung (1786)

Contents

At the Opening and Closing of the Worship Service
Of the Advent of Christ into the Flesh
Of the Incarnation of the Son of God
New Year Hymns
Of the Names and Offices of Christ
Of the Festival of the Epiphany of Christ
Of the Suffering and Death of Jesus Christ
Of the Burial of Jesus Christ
Of the Resurrection of Jesus Christ
Of the Ascension of Jesus Christ
Of the Ascension of Jesus Christ
Of the Holy Ghost and His Gifts
Of the Holy Trinity
Of the Holy Angels

Of the Love of God and of Christ
Of Creation
Of Godly Providence and Government
Of the Word of God
Of Holy Baptism
Of Holy Communion
Of True and False Christendom
Of Human Misery and Corruption
Of True Repentance and Conversion
Of True Faith
Of the Christian Life and Conduct
Of Prayer
Of Spiritual Vigilance
Of Spiritual Struggle and Victory
Of the Union with God and Christ
Of Brotherly and General Love
Of the Imitation of Christ
Of Cross and Suffering
Of the Surrender of the Heart to God
Of Justification
Of True Wisdom
Of God's praise
Of the Lamentation of the Christian Church
Of the Hope of the Christian Church
Of Death and Resurrection
Of the Last Judgement and Damnation
Of Heavenly and Everlasting Life
Morning Hymns
Evening Hymns

Continue next page

Appendix B Cont.

Geistreiches Gesangbuch (1741)

Contents

Of True Wisdom
Of Holy Matrimony
Of the High Exultation of the Believer
Of the Hidden Life of the Believer
Of the Lamentation of Zion
Of the Hope of Zion
Of Death and Resurrection
Of Heaven and the Heavenly Jerusalem
Morning Hymns
Evening Hymns
Table Hymns
In and After Times of General Trouble
Cradle Hymn
Closing Hymn

Erbauliche Liedersammlung (1786)

Contents

Table Hymns
In Times of General Trouble
Travel Hymns

Supplement: Containing hymns that do
    not fit well under previous categories.
    These include, among others:

Pilgrim Hymns
Children's Hymns
Cradle Hymns
Closing Hymn

Appendix C

German Lutheran Hymnbooks in America

Timeline: 1775 — 1800 — 1825 — 1850 — 1875 — 1900 — 1925

Pennsylvania Ministerium
- (1786) Erbauliche Liedersammlung
- (1849) Deutsches Gesangbuch

Tennessee Synod
- (1810) Das Neu Eingerichtete Gesangbuch

Lutheran/Reformed
- (1817) Das Gemeinschaftliche Gesangbuch
- (1849) Neues Gemeinschaftliches Gesangbuch

General Synod
- (1833) Evangelische Liedersammlung

Buffalo Synod
- (1842) Ev. Luth. Kirchengesangbuch

Missouri Synod
- 1847) Kirchengesangbuch

Ohio Synod
- (1870) Gesangbuch für Gemeinden des Ev. Luth. Bekenntnisses

General Council
- (1877) Kirchenbuch

Appendix D

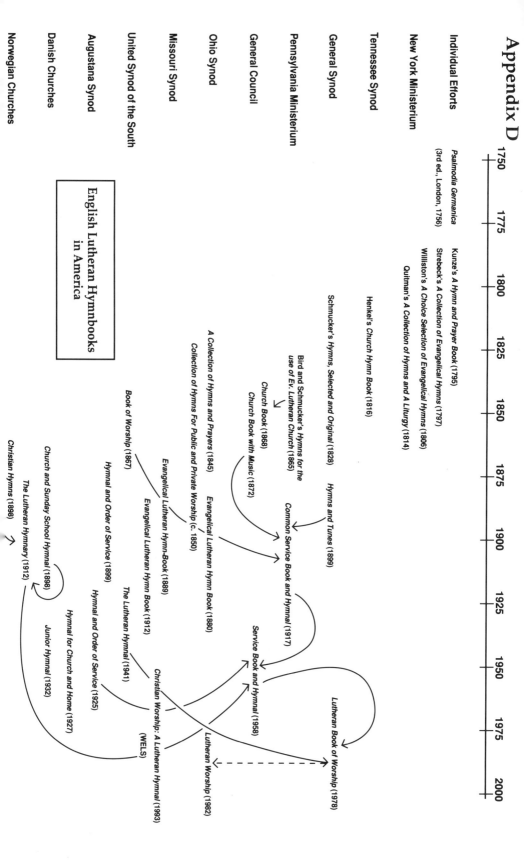

	1750	1775	1800	1825	1850	1875	1900	1925	1950	1975	2000

Individual Efforts — *Psalmodia Germanica* (3rd ed., London, 1756)

New York Ministerium — Kunze's *A Hymn and Prayer Book* (1795); Strebeck's *A Collection of Evangelical Hymns* (1797); Williston's *A Choice Selection of Evangelical Hymns* (1806); Quitman's *A Collection of Hymns and A Liturgy* (1814)

Tennessee Synod — Henkel's *Church Hymn Book* (1816)

General Synod — Schmucker's *Hymns, Selected and Original* (1828)

Pennsylvania Ministerium — Bird and Schmucker's *Hymns for the use of Ev. Lutheran Church* (1865)

General Council — *Church Book* (1868); *Church Book with Music* (1872)

Ohio Synod — *A Collection of Hymns and Prayers* (1845); *Collection of Hymns For Public and Private Worship* (c. 1850)

Missouri Synod

United Synod of the South — *Book of Worship* (1867)

Augustana Synod — *Hymnal and Order of Service* (1899)

Danish Churches — *Church and Sunday School Hymnal* (1898); *Hymnal for Church and Home* (1927)

Norwegian Churches — *Christian Hymns* (1898); *The Lutheran Hymnary* (1912)

Hymns and Tunes (1899)

Common Service Book and Hymnal (1917)

Evangelical Lutheran Hymn-Book (1889)

Evangelical Lutheran Hymn Book (1912)

Evangelical Lutheran Hymn Book (1880)

The Lutheran Hymnal (1941)

Hymnal and Order of Service (1925)

Junior Hymnal (1932)

Service Book and Hymnal (1958)

Lutheran Book of Worship (1978)

Christian Worship: A Lutheran Hymnal (1993) (WELS)

Lutheran Worship (1982)

English Lutheran Hymnbooks in America

Appendix E

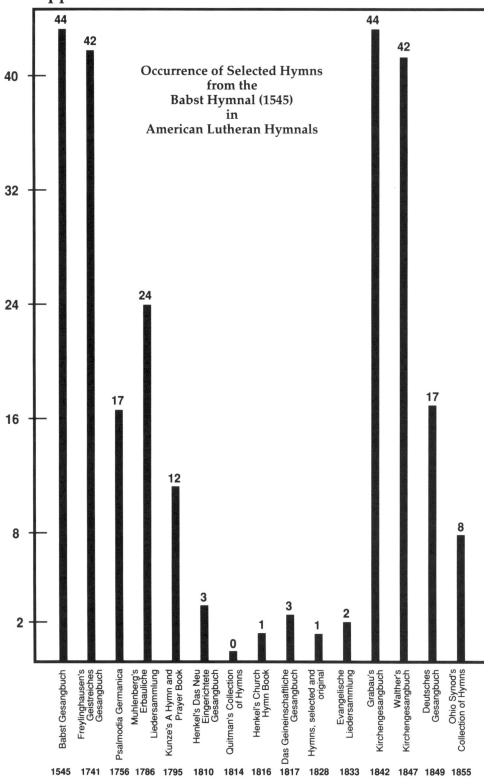

Occurrence of Selected Hymns
from the
Babst Hymnal (1545)
in
American Lutheran Hymnals

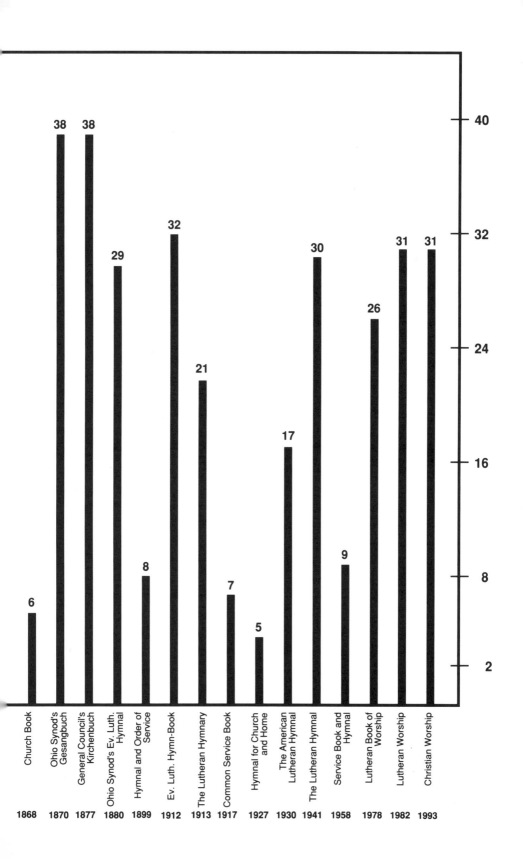

Index

Carl Schalk, lecturer and clinician at numerous church music workshops and pastoral conferences, teaches graduate and undergraduate courses in church music as Distinguished Professor of Music at Concordia University, River Forest, and has been described as "one of the most active lecturers and clinicians on the American church music scene."

He holds advanced degrees from the Eastman School of Music, Rochester, New York (M. Mus.) and from Concordia Seminary, St. Louis, Missouri (M.A.R.). He has received honorary degrees from Concordia College, Seward, Nebraska (LL.D.) and Concordia College, St. Paul, Minnesota (LH.D.), and was named a Fellow of the Hymn Society of the United States and Canada.

He participated in the work leading to the publication of *Lutheran Book of Worship* (1978) and is a well–known composer of choral music, hymn settings for choir and congregation, and hymn tunes that appear in many current hymnals. He was the editor of *Church Music* journal (1966–80). He has served on numerous music boards and committees.

His most recent publications include *Luther on Music: Paradigms of Praise* and *The Praise of God in Song: An Introduction to Christian Hymnody for Congregational Study.*

Dr. Schalk is married to Noel Donata Roeder. They have three grown children.